THAT AMAZING
JUNK-MAN

THAT AMAZING
JUNK-MAN

The Agony and Ecstasy
of a Pastor's Life

TRUMAN H. BRUNK

Foreword by
Myron S. Augsburger

DreamSeeker Books
TELFORD, PENNSYLVANIA

an imprint of
Cascadia Publishing House

Copublished with
Herald Press
Scottdale, Pennsylvania

Cascadia Publishing House orders, information, reprint permissions:
contact@CascadiaPublishingHouse.com
1-215-723-9125
126 Klingerman Road, Telford PA 18969
www.CascadiaPublishingHouse.com

That Amazing Junk-Man
Copyright © 2007 by Cascadia Publishing House.
Telford, PA 18969
All rights reserved
DreamSeeker Books is an imprint of Cascadia Publishing House.
Copublished with Herald Press, Scottdale, PA
Library of Congress Catalog Number:2007002161
ISBN 13: 978-1-931038-44-7; **ISBN 10:** 1-931038-44-9
Book design by Cascadia Publishing House
Cover design by Dawn Ranck

The paper used in this publication is recycled and meets the
minimum requirements of American National Standard for Information Sciences—
Permanence of Paper for Printed Library Materials, ANSI Z39.48-1984.1984

All Bible quotations are used by permission, all rights reserved and unless
otherwise noted are from NIV taken from the Holy Bible, *New International Version®*. Copyright © 1973, 1978, 1984 International Bible Society. All rights reserved
throughout the world. Used by permission of International Bible Society.

Library of Congress Cataloguing-in-Publication Data
Brunk, Truman H., 1931-
That amazing junk-man : the agony and ecstasy of a pastor's life / Truman H.
Brunk ; foreword by Myron S. Augsburger.
    p. cm.
ISBN 978-1-931038-44-7 (5.5 x 8.5" trade pbk. : alk. paper)
1. Mennonite Church. 2. Pastoral theology. 3. Church work. 4. Mennonite
Church--Clergy. 5. Mennonite Church--Sermons. 6. Brunk, Truman H.,
1931- I. Title.
BX8121.3.B78 2007
289.7092--dc22
    [B]

                    2007002161

13 12 11 10 09 08 07   10 9 8 7 6 5 4 3 2 1

To our
children and grandchildren:
Kathleen and Dean Isaacs,
Andrew and Adrienne

Don and Deb Brunk,
Isaac and Caleb

Contents

PART 2: CAP'N JACK

PART 3: BELOVED BROTHER JAMES

Foreword

Stories make history and meaning come alive for us. The author of this work is a good storyteller. *That Amazing Junk-Man* is a good example of "time-binding power"—selecting from the past and channeling it into life again in the present.

There are many preachers who share with words, but not enough who share words with genuine empathy. Truman Brunk is one who is able to empathize, a preacher whose tone and spirit make his words sensitive and inspirational. His insights catch the spirit of Scripture and not just its letter, and his emphases lift the reader to new engagements with truth.

Beginning with the title story, "The Amazing Junk Man," which tells of a person Truman knew as an inspiring presence, and proceeding through a series of stories and sermons, Truman steps into our lives in grace. He invites us to walk with him as together we walk with Jesus in life. Through the insights of history, Truman gives us in the present a still-living prophetic word from the past.

Having walked with Truman Brunk as a colleague in ministry at Eastern Mennonite University and beyond, I have been blessed by his spirit, enriched by his faith, and challenged by his vision. He and his wife Betty have been a refreshing couple in our circle of friends.

I am honored to write this foreword and to recommend this book as a special word of faith from an author who draws stories from over forty years of ministry for Christ. Having been privileged to call Truman to the pastoral role at Eastern Mennonite University, I have rejoiced in his ministry. Now I invite readers likewise to rejoice as Truman empowers us to see in one another the expressions of God's grace.

—*Dr. Myron S. Augsburger*
President Emeritus, Eastern Mennonite University
Harrisonburg, Virginia

Acknowledgments

This book would never have happened without the following persons:

Betty, my beloved mate, was my inspiration and joy throughout. She took my original stories, handwritten on yellow pads, and transformed them into a usable manuscript.

Our long-time friend, Barbara Wenger Borntrager, is creative and smart, "a holy woman," and I like the way she thinks. When I talked to her about this project, she responded with enthusiasm and encouraged me to proceed. Barb took my old sermon notes and brought them to life. The seven sermons in the book were greatly enhanced by Barbara and her editing skills and enthusiastic spirit.

When I met Paul M. Schrock, I knew that I had found my true professional friend. Paul was like a gift from heaven. His guidance and wisdom and counsel were a wonderful blessing and source of strength.

—*Truman H. Brunk*
Harrisonburg, Virginia

Introduction

Psalm 8:5 says of humans that "You made them a little lower than God and crowned them with glory and honor" (NRSV). Indeed

We are amazing human beings.
We create shame and havoc.
But above all else we make astonishing stories,
full of surprises,
full of redemption and salvation.

I am attempting to listen to my own life again for the first time.

These stories come from the lives of sinners and saints. As I reflect on the stories, I am realizing again the great gift of redemption.

Can't you picture God bending low to hear our stories and extend his forgiveness and care? He loves to respond, "You are my beloved child, I am well pleased with you!"

I have come to believe that two groups of people are likely to experience miracles: the very young and the very old. For these, the wall between this life and the next is quite thin. More than at other ages, the old and the young seem to have hearts tuned in and listening. In midlife we seem to be most deaf and unresponsive to God. Make me like young Samuel or like old Simeon! I want to see and hear God! I am looking for thin walls.

I remember the people who have felt the rejection of the church. Their particular chastisement or removal might have happened forty years earlier, but the sting of rejection was still sharp. In camp settings, or even in Sunday morning services, we would sometimes attempt to role-play the original scene. I would offer to play the role of the person who judged or punished. Sometimes healing would take place; sometimes the hoped-for change-of-heart did not follow. Usually some kind of new understanding could be reached.

The stories and miracles in this book are being set to paper for this reason: I would like them to live on as testimony to God's gracious goodness. He loves to take all our broken pieces and make from them something precious. He is That Amazing Junk-Man!

Part 1

WE CALLED
HIM PREACHER TAYLOR

*Stories of Redemption
and Grace*

1

We Called Him Preacher Taylor (*Sermon*)

The unforgettable Jamaican of my boyhood in the Colony.

He came to this country straight from Jamaica when he was a boy.

On Sunday he was a preacher of the gospel.

Six days a week he came through the community collecting junk.

When he would arrive at our place, usually right after lunch, the whole house emptied out to greet him. We all loved this amazing man!

He would preach short excerpts from his Sunday sermon.

He opened his mouth wide when he spoke.

He put his whole body into his preaching.

We never saw that kind of animation in our own church!

At apple picking time, he would grab an empty bushel basket, place it on top of his head, and with perfect balance climb to the top of our twenty-foot ladder. He would start picking apples and pitching them into the basket on his head, then climb down the ladder without touching the basket. For kids who had never been to a carnival or circus, for kids who had never watched TV, what a show this was!

This was wild entertainment! We would clap and cheer! Next would come the tour of the orchard in search of the "junk." We always had something that had fallen off or come loose and needed to be hauled away:

> *An old mowing machine,*
> > *An old wheel or two,*
> > > *Batteries*
> > > > *An engine block*
> > > > > *A pile of rusting, corrugated roofing.*

For Preacher Taylor, everything had some value—twenty-five cents, fifty cents, one dollar, five dollars.

He would load up our junk on the truck, joining our junk with our neighbors' junk. Then off he would go, singing a Jamaican gospel song.

He was an amazing Junk-Man!

My sister Evelyn reminds me of Preacher Taylor. She has an addiction to garage sales. At night she pores over the newspaper sale notices and works up her itinerary for the next day. She rises up early, a woman on a mission, to find some treasure in somebody else's junk.

It is hard to argue with her over that Saturday morning activity when you walk through her house, with its beautiful furniture and accessories—desks, lamps, vases, antique quilts, silverware, chairs.

I ask, "Where did this come from?" (I am thinking, *Did Mom give her this? Did Mom like her better?*) Evelyn is quick to reply, "I found it at a garage sale for three dollars. You should have seen it!"

Evelyn has the vision to see through a thing to its true worth. When she looks at "junk," it's not worthless. She sees the treasure it can become if she takes it home to reclaim and salvage it.

When Evelyn gets her "junk" home, she puts it in the garage to brood over. To envision and dream. She can take an old picture frame covered with chipped antique white paint, apply a little paint remover and sand paper, and find a beautiful walnut frame. Everybody else thinks *junk*. Evelyn thinks *treasure*. She loves to raise things to a new life. What a gift!

Almighty God is in the business of reclaiming and salvaging lost and broken people.

God is in the business of seeing
    through pain,
      adversity,
        our mistakes and our sins,

All the things that throw us onto the junk heap of life and cause us
    to think:
    I am no good.
      I am worthless.
        I am sick.

God sees through ALL of this. He sees what we can BECOME!
    He has an eye for
      Redemption,
        Restoration,
          Raising us to new life!

The Bible is full of examples:
God going down to Egypt and walking among a people of social
    discards,
      Beaten and bruised,
        The light gone out of their eyes.

God saw through to what they would become:
    A people of virtue.
      A people of faith.
        A light in the world.

There's Rahab, the prostitute.

> *Society had discarded her to the junk heap of life.*
> *But God came and saw a treasure.*
> *He saw the woman of faith that she would become.*

In the New Testament Jesus came to walk among us, saying,
> *"Today salvation has come to this house. For the Son of*
> *man came to seek and to save the lost."*

Jesus saw Simon Peter and Andrew, his brother, fishing.
> *He saw through . . . to the treasure they could become.*
> *And he called, "Come, follow Me."*
> *He labored over them——his projects.*
> *And they became treasures.*
> *He would even die for them.*

Think of the twelve disciples.

People would say, "Matthew can never be spiritual. He's just a
> *greedy, money-loving tax collector."*

Jesus said, "I see treasure. A man of faith. He will become my
> *disciple."*

All through Jesus' ministry, He went through Galilee, proclaiming
> *Good News.*
> *They brought to him all the sick.*
> *Those who were afflicted with diseases, pain, demons,*
> > *and he saw what they would become."*
> > *The woman at the well.*
> > *Zacchaeus.*
> > > *The woman who touched the*
> > > *hem of his garment.*
> > > *The blind, the mute.*
> > > > *The man with the withered hand.*
> > > > *The woman taken in adultery.*

Someone came from heaven.
A heavenly Junk-Man.
> *To seek out treasures.*
> *To redeem and raise them to new life.*

Believe in That Amazing Junk-Man!
  He sees through all the chaos, the sin, the mistakes.
  What I have done to hurt others.
  What others have done to me.

He sees the infinite value of one broken doll, cast out on the junk
  heap of life.
And he says, "I will make her new!
  I will raise him to new life!
  I will breathe my Spirit into them."

He sees the treasure!
He is the Great Redeemer!
I am a salvage project.

And those redeeming hands reach out,
  Touch,
    Love,
      Heal.

What an Amazing Junk-Man!

Preacher Taylor was the father of Naomi Francisco. Naomi married Leslie Francisco, now deceased, and is lovingly called the mother of Calvary Mennonite Church in Hampton, Virginia.

2

Precious Lord, Take My Hand (Sermon)

My dad leads a sinner to peace and salvation

William and Sarah were some of our closest neighbors. When things were going well, William was a wonderful husband and father, neighbor, and church member. But at times he would fall into old patterns of drinking, then "all hell would break loose." William was an alcoholic.

William and Sarah and their children had moved to the Colony during World War II. They were among the many out-of-state families who came to find work in the Newport News Shipyard. First the men would come without their families and would board in homes near the shipyard. My parents kept a number of these men.

After the war, they stayed on in these good-paying jobs, attended our church, and made a huge contribution to our community. Because of these early "boarders," my father kept a close connection with the out-of-staters. I think he admired their simple, hardworking, humble ways. They were real people!

Alcohol took its toll on William, and he developed cancer in his throat and mouth. His condition worsened. Finally, William lay in a deep coma in the hospital. Dad came to the room to give comfort to Sarah.

Sarah said, "If only William could wake up enough to pray I would feel so much better." Dad believed in prayer. He stood at the bedside and prayed aloud that if William needed to make things right, God would waken him one last time.

William's eyes opened and Dad invited him to pray aloud, "Forgive my sin and save my soul." William repeated this prayer four times, then fell back into the coma, and his breathing stopped.

That evening my father phoned me in Pennsylvania and told me the story. I was moved. I said, "Dad, this is a miracle! Please write your prayer and send it to me." Here is the prayer I received a few days later:

Dear God in heaven, here is William hanging between life and death.
Dear Lord, if there is more he could do for preparation for moving into eternity, please revive him for that preparation.
I pray that he might die in the trust of salvation from Jesus the Savior,
and that by your grace he might enter into that eternal trust.
Bless and keep his companion.
We pray for William's children and grandchildren whom he loves so much.
Please comfort them and guide them in the way of righteousness and eternal salvation.
Thank you for your love and caring.
Amen

Some of our journey is in the dark. God comes to us, tenderly lifts us in his arms, and carries us home. This story reminds me of the song we love to sing, "Precious Lord, Take My Hand," which movingly invites our precious Lord to lead us, though weak and worn, though in storm or night, to the light and home.

My father's ministry was not accidental—it was intentional. He was "being Jesus" to William. Here is what Jesus taught about prayer and forgiveness, and what Jesus said of his own ministry:

> It is not the healthy who need a doctor, but the sick. But go and learn what this means: I desire mercy, not sacrifice. For I have not come to call the righteous, but sinners. (Matt. 9:12, 13)

Jesus demonstrated this message to—
The Leper
  The paralyzed servant
    Peter's mother-in-law
      The demoniac
        The paralytic
          The outcasts
            The poor and broken
              The battered lambs and
                lost sheep.

Many religious leaders of Jesus' day were afraid to connect with sinners. But Jesus taught that a truly merciful person is not endangered by such contact. Contact brings healing to both the sinner and the healer. When holiness encounters sin, sin is put to flight.

Recall the woman who touched the hem of his garment. Jesus turned, "Who touched me? I felt life flow from me!"

St. Francis of Assisi, before his conversion from a religious life of privilege and position to a life of mercy, felt sick inside every time he saw a leper from a distance. The leper was broken, emaciated, hands and feet globs of rotting flesh—repulsive.

After being touched by mercy, Francis one day met a leper. Instead of walking away from him, he met him in full embrace and kissed his broken, rotting flesh.

"In that moment," said he, "I heard the divine whisper, 'I desire mercy, not sacrifice.'"

How can we have such a conversion of our own beliefs? Do we have a "litany of religion" like many religious leaders of Jesus' day? Could our litany turn to mercy and compassion?

I have a litany of being religious. I attend service faithfully.
I belong to a Sunday school class, prayer group, committees.
I tend the nursery, I lead a small group.
   And inside I feel dull and sometimes critical,
   A kind of hypocritical devoutness.
   I plod through religious exercises.
   I don't feel the white-hot fire of the Holy Spirit.
I want mercy to be the cornerstone of my life.
I want to be on a mercy mission!
I want Christ to be central.

Before I leave this building today, I will meet someone who needs
      mercy.
   A loving word, a touch that heals.

As I drive home, someone on the way needs mercy.
   The driver ahead of me, going 20 mph in a 45 zone.
   He needs prayer instead of frustration.

When I enter my house, someone needs mercy.
   My own spouse, my child, with longings and loneliness.

At work this week, someone who is hurting,
   Broken on the wheels of life, needing someone to say, "You
      matter to me."

My father offered mercy to William. In that moment, both William and my dad experienced the miracle of God's grace.

   The Spirit of the Lord is on me,
      because he has anointed me
      to preach good news to the poor.
   He has sent me to proclaim freedom for
      the prisoners

and recovery of sight for the blind,
to release the oppressed,
to proclaim the year of the Lord's favor.
—Luke 4:18-19

3

A Walled Garden

*A pack of Kools leads me
into youthful indiscretions.*

For children growing up in the walled paradise of the Colony, every precaution was taken to keep out SIN. We were not allowed to attend movies or ball games, were not supposed to go to the bowling alley, and were warned against going to a circus or a carnival.

We *were* allowed to roller skate on our macadam roads, and I always looked forward to the nights when the young people arranged a roller-skating party. When I was about thirteen, I was at one of these skating parties when the unexpected happened: I saw, lying along the edge of the road, a pack of Kool cigarettes! I should have skated on by, but I couldn't make myself leave that pack of Kools on the ground. I stooped to pick up the pack and put it in my jacket pocket.

At home I hid the cigarettes in my dresser drawer. In the coming days they were always on my mind. What would it be like to stand holding a cigarette between two fingers and puff away, with smoke rising? Wouldn't I be sophisticated!

Finally I could wait no longer. I found matches, pulled out the pack, and headed behind the chicken house. I smoked one cigarette, then another, then the whole pack. I felt like a

worldly man. At last I was a grown-up sinner—with a big secret!

How did Dad find out? I don't know, but that night he
asked, "Have you been smoking cigarettes?" I had to admit my
guilt. He was disappointed by my flagrant misbehavior. He
must have given it a lot of thought because, not long afterward,
he confronted me again. He said, "It's clear that Warwick High
School has been a bad influence on you. Mama and I have decided that you will transfer to Eastern Mennonite High School
in Harrisonburg."

I was allowed to finish the year, under close supervision.
The next year I became a dormitory student in the Valley. I
never smoked another cigarette in my life.

For a good many years I felt guilty for the pain I had caused
my parents. I remember overhearing a beloved aunt reassuring
my dad that she was pretty sure I would turn out all right.
Much later I came across a secret, and maybe this was the reason Dad had reacted as he did: During his teen years my dad
had smoked! My perfect dad! I am convinced that "No one is
righteous, no not one."

> *James 1:14-16.* But one is tempted by one's own desire,
> being lured and enticed by it; then, when that desire has
> conceived, it gives birth to sin, and that sin, when it is
> fully grown, gives birth to death. Do not be deceived,
> my beloved.

My Mother's Song

*After fifty years, my parents take
the siblings to the grave of their firstborn.*

My Dear, Do you know, how a long time ago,
Two poor little babes, whose names I don't know,
Were stolen away, on a fine summer's day,
And lost in the woods, I've heard people say.

And when it was night, so sad was their plight,
The sun it went down, And the moon gave no light.
They sobbed and they sighed, and bitterly cried,
And the poor little things, they lay down and died.

And when they were dead, the robins so red
Brought strawberry leaves and over them spread:
And all the day long, they sung them this song:
Poor babes in the wood, poor babes in the wood.

My mother would hold me on her lap, rocking and singing. She sang a lot of different songs, but this is one I remember to this day. It was such a sad song. Years and years later I came to believe that she was singing this song not only for me and my sisters; she was also singing it for Baby Delsie.

Mom and Dad lost their first baby while they were living in Washington, D.C. The baby lived for only a few hours. Mom had not been able to go to the burial of her little one—Dad and the funeral director went alone to a little cemetery and placed the tiny coffin in the ground. Dad cried for a long time before he left the grave, and he was still weeping when he returned to Mom's bedside. They held each other close and cried together.

Fifty years later the story came alive for me. My parents expressed a desire to have their children visit the grave-site with them. We drove together. Leaving Old River Road (now 52nd Ave.) we turned onto a quiet street and parked the car.

With Dad leading the way, we climbed up a steep and rugged hillside, through briars and undergrowth and old gnarly trees, and came to a tiny cemetery in the woods. We could make out the grave-stones of a few graves, and Dad walked over to the iron frame of a child's crib, anchored in the ground. Wild strawberries covered the ground.

This was a piece of history he did not want to neglect. Dad wanted the family to know the resting place of our little sister. A few more years went by, and Dad went back to Washington to erect a proper grave marker. Working alone, he pulled the heavy material up the hillside, mixed the concrete, and placed the granite stone, carved with his first child's name—Delsie Brunk. It was something he had to do before he went to his heavenly home, where he holds little Delsie in loving arms.

5

Peggy, Steve, and Sandra

*One family tragedy makes way
for two family blessings.*

Sunday morning about 9:45, I had just read the opening
Scripture for Sunday school and dismissed those gathered
in the sanctuary to form their separate classes. I looked toward
the side entrance of the church, the door that leads to the ante-
room, and saw my father beckoning me to come.

I knew immediately that something was wrong. With tears
he told me that my sister Peggy had been in an automobile accident. On the way home from her night duty at Eastern State
Hospital she had apparently fallen asleep, her car had rolled up-
side-down into shallow water, and she had drowned.

Our family was shattered. For months we endured in a
state of shock. We were such a small family, with only three
children—Evelyn, Peggy, and me. Peggy was the youngest in
the family and so easy to love. As a child she was cuddly, warm,
and tender. Mom and Dad called her pet names like "Peg-
Nest."

Peggy and I had been the closest of buddies since baby-
hood. Just eighteen months apart in age, we formed a bond that

kept others out. We spoke the same language and understood each other while the rest of the family could not figure out what we were saying. Many of our family photos show Peggy and me side-by-side, arms around each other riding in a wagon, or holding hands on the front porch.

A family never gets over such a loss. The grief never goes away. Peggy was twenty-six at the time of her death, married, with a six-month-old son, Steve, her pride and joy. She and Steve's father, Elwood Brydge, worked opposite shifts at Eastern State Hospital to take turns being with the baby. They lived next to our parents, who also helped care for their grandson.

From that time on, Steve was raised by his grandparents. He spent time with his father, but the primary care fell on his grandparents, my parents. My folks had always longed for more children. Their first baby died at birth, then they had three more children. By the time Peggy and I were in our teens, Sandy, age three, joined the family.

Sandy was a pretty little thing, expressive, smart, and talented. She brought added joy and laughter into the house. Now with Peggy's tragic departure, Mom and Dad had another little one to rear.

Steve grew into a boisterous, rambunctious boy. He would ram his tricycle into doors and walls and leave his mark everywhere. We called him our little Bulldozer. Always center-stage, he thrived in the limelight. By the time he was two, Betty and I were having our own children, and these three cousins—Steve, Kathy, and Don—were lively playmates.

When Steve became a teenager my father, now in his seventies, dug out his old carpentry tools, and the two of them built a house to put on the market. When it sold, they built another. The two shared the profits. They made quite a team. Dad lived to be ninety-two, and I have always believed that he lived an extra ten years because he wanted to be there for Steve.

When Peggy died, we were left holding a treasure. Now her son, who has been raised as my brother/nephew, is a gift to my own family and to the church and community. Steve and Becky have four children who are almost grown. They live just a few miles from us. Sandy and her husband Nevin Steiner also live nearby.

Mom and Dad have joined Peggy in heaven, but their loving presence remains with us. God redeems our sadness in surprising ways.

6

The Trail West

As Civil War Virginia "deserters,"
my ancestors almost died in Kansas.

The story of my great-grandparents, Henry G. and Susan Heatwole Brunk, breaks my heart whenever it is told or read to me.

When my own family traveled west in the summer of 1973 we made a special effort to meet relatives in the Kansas area where my great-grandparents had dreamed of living. A gracious relative and host was Dr. Florence Cooprider Friesen, living in Hesston, Kansas.

When she learned of our interest in the family story, she decided she would be our tour guide. She drove with us to the place near Newton, Kansas. She helped us find the grave markers and our family of four, including two pre-teens, stood in the tiny cemetery beside a busy highway (the Santa Fe Trail). Dr. Friesen held in her hands a booklet, *Story of Grandmother Heatwole-Brunk-Cooprider*, by Ethel Estella (Cooprider) Erb, and said, "You stand right here while I read this to you." Much of the following is from her reading that day.

What a happy day it was when Susan and Baby Sarah were united with Henry in Hagerstown. But this was not a safe place—the Rebel army came to Hagerstown looking for "deserters," and finally Henry and R. J. Heatwole, Susan's brother, decided they needed to move again. They settled in Illinois, and five more children were added to the Brunk household. But the two men had another destination in mind.

Land was being offered to homesteaders in Kansas, and it was the dream of the two brothers-in-law to move west and stake out their prairie land side by side. Uncle R. J., a single man, went on ahead, bought his land, and started his home. Henry and Susan and their six children would take a slower pace in their prairie schooner.

Besides all the other dangers of the trail, there was never enough water. Settlers were reluctant to share safe water, and the travelers were forced to drink from ponds and streams. They finally reached their promised homestead, next to Reuben, but by now Henry was sick with typhoid fever.

Henry unharnessed his horses, turned them to graze, set up a crude shelter, in wigwam fashion, and went to bed. In eight days he was dead. The whole family was sick. Just thirty-six days later, little Henry G. Jr., was born. Thirteen days after that, five-year-old Fanny died. In three more days, December 22, eleven-year-old Sarah, the oldest child, died. The following April, baby Henry G. died.

Grandmother thought perhaps God, in his mercy, would take them all. Still living were Joseph, Henrietta, Minnie, and George R, ages eight, six, four, and two. At one point Little George was given up to die also, with the thought "not to punish him anymore with medicine, but just lay him quietly off to the side, and let him die in peace."

Little George lived! But instead of the happy family and the home his parents had dreamed of, there were four graves on the southwest corner of the prairie quarter section, and one little grave back in Virginia.

George, my grandfather, would later recall his earliest memory of standing beside his mother as she cut up her husband's clothing to clothe her children. He remembered his mother weeping, and he wept too, hiding his face in the folds of her skirt.

Sometimes, sitting in my comfortable, almost luxurious surroundings, I remember the hard times and trials of my ancestors who wouldn't give up, and I marvel that I am even here.

7

A Determined Great-Grandmother

The bridge was burning! She found the shallowest place and forded the river.

One family story has come down through the generations and still has a strong impact on my life. In recent years the lessons in this story have become even more precious to me.

My great-grandfather, Henry G. Brunk, was born and raised in Virginia's Shenandoah Valley. During the Civil War, all able-bodied Valley men were expected to join the Confederate army. But my great-grandfather, raised Mennonite , was a conscientious objector and refused military service.

He was taken to Richmond, Virginia, and given three choices: He could put on the uniform and take up arms; he could haul provisions for the army (noncombatant work); or he could be put into prison. Along with some of his friends, he chose noncombatant work, and his duties included taking care of the sick soldiers and hauling hay for the cavalry horses.

After a time, Great-Grandfather came to believe that his noncombatant work was actually part of the killing machinery, and he knew he could not continue in this helping role. So one day, in the process of hauling hay, he left his team and walked through the orchards and woods and headed back to the Valley. From then on, he was labeled a deserter with a price on his head.

He knew he could not return to his wife and baby son, so when he arrived in the Valley, friends and neighbors hid him in their attics. After two-and-a-half years living as a fugitive, he joined sixteen other young men. At great peril, they made their way across the mountains of Virginia and West Virginia, crossing the Mason Dixon line into the "free" state of Maryland.

Henry sent word for his young wife Susan to come to Hagerstown. Estella Cooprider Erb tells the story.

> Susan and baby daughter started with a horse and spring wagon for the place her husband had named. Her sister accompanied her, with their few possessions, in a one-horse wagon. The course followed between the two armies, moving northward as the Union army fell back. They braved the dangers of fording rushing waters . . . at one time driving through army lines.
>
> The soldiers halted her and seized her faithful horse; she bravely asked them to leave hands off her horse. As they were unhitching, she clung to the bridle. Just at this moment came the cry, "Yanks! Yanks!" The soldiers left the horse to flee from the coming enemy.
>
> At Harpers Ferry, where Susan needed to cross the Potomac River, the bridge was burning! She found the shallowest place and forded the river. She drove into Hagerstown, looking right and left, and suddenly halted. She spotted her husband in the window of a shoe-repair shop—and they were reunited!

Family stories keep families united. They nourish our souls. On my seventieth birthday I visited Harpers Ferry and spoke to the guide. When I showed her my little book of history, she asked if she could make a copy for the archives at Harpers Ferry. The story of Susan Heatwole Brunk lives on.

The foundations of my spiritual life were laid long before I was born. I thank God for a godly heritage!

8

Two Strong Grandfathers

Larger-than-life leaders at Eastern Mennonite School

It's a wonder that my parents ever survived the turbulent years of their courtship. If they had let their fathers dictate for them, they may have gone their separate ways. Fortunately for me, they had enough good judgment to follow their hearts.

Ruth Smith and Truman Brunk met at Eastern Mennonite School (now Eastern Mennonite University) in Harrisonburg, Virginia, in 1920. Ruth was a daughter of Jacob (J. B.) and Lena (Burkhart) Smith, and Truman was the eldest son of George R. and Katie (Wenger) Brunk.

George R. was a founding father of the school and had been influential in bringing J. B. from Kansas to be its first president. But after just a few years of Grandfather Smith's tenure, there arose a storm around musical instruments. Grandfather Brunk wanted musical instruments banished from campus, and he was determined that faculty should not have musical instruments in their homes.

My mother's journals tell about the wonderful times she and Dad had together—climbing Massanutten Peak, hiking up Mole Hill, ice-skating on nearby ponds, and playing tennis on school-grounds. But her journals also reflect the rising tension between the school administrators and the board. Grandfather Smith had a nice piano in his home. His wife and children enjoyed music, and some of the family members were talented musicians.

My sister tells me that Grandfather Smith had perfect pitch. My mother taught us the hymn, "A Call For Help," written by her father and published in the *Church and Sunday School Hymnal*. President Smith was not convinced that he should get rid of the piano. Instead, he accepted termination of his appointment, and moved his family to Ohio. I had never heard this story until I myself was a student at Eastern Mennonite College.

I am proud of both grandfathers. Grandfather Smith (1870-1951) was a small man with a huge intellect. When he came of age, his parents presented him with the same choice they offered all their children —a farm or an education. I am so glad he chose an education. From the cover of one of his books, I have copied the following:

> He attended schools at Elkhart, Indiana; Ohio Northern University in Ada, Ohio; Temple University in Philadelphia, Pennsylvania, and Oskaloosa College, Oskaloosa, Iowa, where he received the M.A and D.D. degrees. He was ordained to the ministry in 1897 and held pastorates in Missouri and Ohio. He served as a minister, educator and writer in the Mennonite Church from the time of his ordination until his death on September 23, 1951. He served on the faculty of Hesston College, Hesston, Kansas, teaching Bible, history and Greek. He was the president of Eastern Mennonite College in Harrisonburg, Virginia, 1917 to 1922, where he also taught Bible, Greek and Hebrew.

Grandfather George R. Brunk (1871-1938) also had a huge intellect and was large in stature. He grew up on the

Kansas prairies with his widowed mother. When she remarried, the family situation became uncomfortable for the teenager, and he was sent to live in a small cabin. This was a lonely period for him. He became a serious student of the Bible and began a program of self-education he continued all his life. He loved to study the Bible. He was a respected preacher in the West and was invited to hold evangelistic meetings in churches across the country.

In his mid-twenties, he traveled to the Shenandoah Valley of Virginia for revival meetings and, according to family lore, from the pulpit he noticed a young woman rise to get a cup of water for her mother. He leaned over and asked the host preacher who that young woman was. After the service, he was introduced to Katie Wenger, and six weeks later they were married.

George and Katie settled in Kansas where they started their family. My father, Truman, was one of three children born while the family lived in Kansas. After George and Katie moved to Denbigh, Virginia, six more children were born.

I am happy to say that my two grandfathers grew to respect and appreciate each other. They were both conservative theologians and usually agreed on their interpretations of the Bible. I am also glad that their differences did not deter my parents. Mom and Dad were married in the home of Bishop John M. Shenk in Elida, Ohio.

At first Grandfather Brunk held his new daughter-in-law at arm's length. He thought the way she dressed and the way she combed her hair were "too worldly." What he would learn was that my mother had paved the way for my father to build a strong faith in God. It was through my mother that Dad came back into the fold. Grandfather Brunk eventually accepted Mom warmly into the family.

After Grandfather Smith left Eastern Mennonite School, he continued pastoral work. He was pastor at Salem Mennonite Church in Elida, Ohio, and also traveled extensively, lecturing and preaching. His first love was prophecy and the Book of Revelation. I remember the huge charts on the walls that he would use in his teaching.

To earn a living for his large family, he raised and sold potatoes. When we went to visit our Ohio grandparents, I would see Grandfather pushing his potato cart through the Elida streets.

But, unlike other farmers, when evening came, Grandfather's day was just getting started. He often stayed up until three in the morning, studying and writing. His two major books were the *Greek-English Concordance of the New Testament* and *A Revelation of Jesus Christ.*

Once my mother asked him how bad it was to be asked to leave Eastern Mennonite School and take his family to the farm in Ohio. He replied that it was a great relief! As an administrator, he had no time to write, and after he settled on the farm, he could finally work at his first love, that of writing.

Waiting

Not only through earth's toilsome years
Do parents watch and wait
For children scattered far;
But having heard the Master call,
And having folded earth work all aside
And gone away,
The vigil is not ended;
The soul-fire of love still burns within;
In that far land they wait and wait,
For the children to come home.
—George R. Brunk

A Call for Help

At home and abroad, on life's battlefield,
Brave soldiers are needed their service to yield
For Jesus who died that all might have life.
Come enter the battle, be bold in the strife.

Refrain:
The trumpet is sounding, we're off to the fray,
Immanuel's banner we'll lift up today.
Then onward, still onward in his name we go,
Till all of his creatures the Lord's name will know.

Our Captain is calling for volunteers now,
Let all to his mandates submissively bow;
Not life and not friends let any hold dear
While cries of the needy break out on your ear.

Oh, who then will go in the strength of the Lord,
Uplifting his banner, proclaiming his word?
Who will help to redeem dying souls from the grave,
In telling of Jesus the mighty, to save?
—J. B. Smith

9

A Faithful Pioneer Evangelist and Hymn-Writer

Under John S. Coffman, far removed,
my grandfathers accepted Christ.

Both of my grandfathers came to salvation through the preaching of John S. Coffman. This pioneer evangelist and hymn-writer, born in Rockingham County, Virginia, traveled widely and spoke with such passion that he melted hard hearts. He would extend his hand and invite seekers to come and take his hand.

In the book about Grandfather Brunk, *Faithfully, Geo. R.,* author J. C. Wenger notes, "It was a happy day when he [George] yielded his life to Christ under the ministry of John S. Coffman." He was seventeen years old, living in Kansas.

Following his conversion, Grandfather experienced a time of despair and uncertainty. But with the help and loving guidance of his uncle, R. J. Heatwole, Grandfather spoke of being "brightly saved" and never again doubted his salvation.

In the book, *His Name Was John*, the story of John S. Coffman is told by Barbara Coffman, his granddaughter. She describes evangelistic meetings held in Ontario, Canada. When young Jacob Schmidt (later known as J. B. Smith) was invited to attend, Jacob replied, "Just count me out, brother. You won't get me up there."

However, later that evening he sat in the congregation and was deeply stirred by the message. When the invitation was given, Grandfather Smith "rushed down the aisle." As he rounded the heating stove, he tripped over the stove and landed in the lap of a lady seated in the aisle. Nothing could stop him now that he was giving his life to the Lord!

Following are the words of a song written by John S. Coffman for use in evangelistic services. I like to think this beautiful song appealed to the hearts of my two grandfathers then as it does to me today:

O weary wanderer, come home, Thy Savior bids thee come,
Thou long in sin didst love to roam, Yet still He calls thee, come.
Think of thy Father's house today, So blest with plenteous store;
Think of thy sinful, wandering way, Then come, and roam no
*   more.*
Poor prodigal, come home and rest, Come and be reconciled;
Here lean upon thy Father's breast, He loves His wandering child.

Refrain:
Help me, dear Savior, Thee to own, And ever faithful be;
And when thou sittest on thy throne, O Lord, remember me.

10

A State Champion

"Lord, you can have my running, too."

When I arrived at Eastern Mennonite College in the 1960s, intercollegiate athletics was in its infancy. Even so, we had our winners at the state level. One athlete who stood out from the rest was Elton Horst, a long distance runner. He won state recognition for three straight years.

It was a welcome distraction to take a break from work or studies and walk down to the track to watch the runners compete. At the beginning of the race, Elton was just one of the pack—they would run in a tight cluster into the woods and disappear from sight. Minutes later the runners emerged, with Elton well in the lead. I loved to watch and cheer him on to victory.

Elton had made a commitment to memorize Bible passages as he ran. During his long hours of practice, hours of isolation, he memorized Scripture. He became known on campus for both his running and his Bible memory work. He had tremendous influence on other students, particularly athletes. Who wouldn't want to be like Elton?

During the 1960s and 1970s, Spiritual Life Week occurred twice each year—in the fall and again in the spring. Powerful evangelists like Tom Skinner, David Seamands, and Don Jacobs would preach and invite students and faculty to a closer walk with Christ.

On one occasion, when the invitation was given, Elton came walking down the aisle. I will always remember the moment of meeting Elton, offering him my hand, and kneeling to pray with him. I heard him say, "Lord, you can have my running, too."

Elton continued to run as a champion athlete, but now his goals were broader and higher. Now as I watched him run, I was often reminded of the words of Kierkegaard: "Purity is to will one thing for your life." Elton had found the "one thing."

A Covenant Prayer in the Wesleyan Tradition

I am no longer my own, but thine.
Put me to what thou wilt, rank me with whom thou wilt.
Put me to doing, put me to suffering.
Let me be employed by thee or laid aside for thee,
exalted for thee or brought low for thee.
Let me be full, let me be empty.
Let me have all things, let me have nothing.
I freely and heartily yield all things to thy pleasure and disposal.
And now, O glorious and blessed God,
thou art mine, and I am thine.
So be it.
And the covenant which I have made on earth,
let it be ratified in heaven.
Amen.
—John Wesley

11

Aunt Ruth
Finds Her Match

*She was the most dynamic,
lively person I ever knew.*

Once when I was about five years old, our family went to see Grandfather and Grandmother Brunk. Aunt Ruth came strolling through the living room, carrying a candy bar. It was the first candy bar I had ever seen, and it was a Baby Ruth. Ever since, whenever I see a Baby Ruth candy bar I think of my aunt.

Aunt Ruth was the most dynamic, lively person I knew. Capable and independent, she was almost bigger than life. Our family wondered if she would ever find a husband to be her match. But when she introduced us to Grant Stoltzfus, we could tell he was intelligent. She had found her equal!

They married and started their family. While Grant worked on his academic pursuits, Ruth continued with her own calling. She was the founder of Heart to Heart, a radio program sponsored by Mennonite Media. Even now, when Aunt Ruth is ninety, I still hear her recorded messages on the local radio station.

While I was attending seminary part-time and working as pastor of students full-time at Eastern Mennonite, Grant's office was just down the hall from mine. If I needed an article on a particular subject, I could ask Grant, and he would go to his files, which were jammed with information at his fingertips. He was a resource to many of his students and fellow-faculty.

Grant was a radical follower of Jesus. His faith dictated how he lived his life. The first year we worked together, I wanted to vote for the first time in my life. I heard Grant say, "I always vote as if I were poor and black." This continues to be my beacon. On the way to the polls, I remember Grant and use his words as my guiding light.

He had a great sense of humor and could laugh at himself. Everybody knew he was the absent-minded professor. His family told a story of the time they traveled on the Pennsylvania Turnpike and Grant needed to use the rest room. He drove into the next service area, went inside to take care of his needs, and came out with a little package of crackers.

As he handed the crackers around, he said, "My mother taught me to always make some little purchase if you need to use the facilities." But five miles down the turnpike, he ran out of gas!

In his fifties, Grant was mowing the lawn when he had a heart attack and died. This vital, thoughtful, inspiring, and loving man was no longer with us. The world would never be the same. Eastern Mennonite would not be the same. No one could replace Grant. Grant's five children were in their teens and twenties when he died.

The children had all inherited their father's unconventional ways and sense of humor. They decided that Grant would not want an expensive, factory-built casket. They would build the casket themselves. They called and asked if I would help. All day we labored at the task, talking about Dad and how much he would appreciate what we were doing.

When the carpentry work was finished, the girls brought fine fabric for lining the casket. Then one of the children got the idea that we should each take a ride in the casket, just to test it out. One by one, we climbed into the box and were carried for a ride around the yard.

Aunt Ruth and her family grieved for a long time. It seemed like they could never get past their loneliness and missing their husband and father. Aunt Ruth continued with her writing and her holy work. She had her international students and their families living in her apartments and looking to her for advice and resources.

When our son Don needed a home away from home, he was welcome at Aunt Ruth's door. I remember one time, during a family discussion around the dinner table, we mentioned Aunt Ruth and her hospitality and her many projects. Don said, "The world needs more women like Aunt Ruth." I say amen, amen, and amen!

12

A Search for Meaning

*The young mother's six-month-old
"little cosmic freak!"*

I accepted an invitation to Lower Deer Creek Church in Iowa. It was late spring and the rolling cornfields were lush and green. Every day I walked in the countryside and felt renewed in mind and body and soul.

When evening came, we would gather in the church for the sermon. Sometimes a person would ask to have individual conversation, and I welcomed this kind of personal interaction.

One day a young mother came to talk. I would describe her as a Sixties-type person. Some people called them hippies or flower children. Her name was Madelaine and she seemed to me a sophisticated and intelligent young woman.

She was attracted to the unsophisticated, modest folk in our church community. She marveled at their care for each other—and the care that flowed out to include her and her young family.

We talked about foundations of faith—how faith is built and how it can be passed on to our children. The "God Is Dead" movement was making its way through intellectual circles, and Madelaine was in a questioning stage. She had no foundation on which to build.

The whole time we talked, she held her six-month-old baby on her lap. At one point she bounced the little one on her knees and said, "You poor little cosmic freak! Where did you come from?"

I have often wondered whatever happened to this mother and child. By now the child would be nearing thirty. Where are they now? Are they still wandering aimlessly across the earth?

The Scriptures say, "They will know Christ by our love for one another." I believe the witness of Lower Deer Creek Church in Iowa helped this young mother find the truth. We are not cosmic freaks. We are sons and daughters of a loving God. This is the foundation of our faith.

Matthew 7:24-25. Everyone then who hears these words of mine and acts on them will be like a wise man who built his house on rock. The rain fell, the floods came, and the winds blew and beat on that house, but it did not fall, because it had been founded on rock.

13

The Library Drive of '69

*"What if a holy fire ignited us
and set our community ablaze?"*

I had no clue that the week would be the most dramatic of my life. By now I had been campus pastor for four years, loved my work, couldn't imagine a place of service more invigorating and rewarding. On this particular Thursday morning I walked along with the body of students and faculty toward the auditorium for daily chapel and overheard two librarians ahead of me saying, "We have lost the library."

Their voices and body language held deep sadness. The college was desperate for a new library, and we believed it was an act of faith to proceed with plans to move out of the cramped space in the old Administration Building. Blueprints had been drawn for a beautiful facility, and a federal grant was secured with the agreement that the college would raise matching funds.

Development staff had labored long and hard and the student body had responded generously to a fund drive, but we had come up short. The Board of Directors had announced that we would not proceed with the million-dollar library until we had every dollar in hand, and we were $111,000 short!

With morning chapel on my mind, I hurried on ahead to be sure all was ready for the day's program. But I felt gripped by a thought that would not go away: *What if a holy fire ignited us, filled us with the Spirit, and set our community ablaze?*

The minute chapel was finished I caught up with student leader Ev Ressler. He too caught the excitement. Together we found Bruce Yoder, and that evening the three of us met with about twenty student leaders, determined to organize a drive that would raise the necessary funds.

Everybody seemed ablaze with inspiration. We would announce a bake sale and public auction. We would drive to Lancaster for food to sell at the auction. We would advertise student labor for cleaning out chicken houses. One idea kindled another. Everybody seemed baptized with passion and fire. Would the fire catch on? Would the student body and the community ignite?

By chapel time Friday morning we were ready to spread the word. The flame caught, and spread, and could not be contained. The whole community became fully engaged. The college gym became the hub of activity. Somebody painted a thermometer to depict the dollars contributed, and the lines advanced all that day and night.

For three days and three nights some of us did not sleep. There were phone calls to make, trips to take. Housewives stayed in their kitchens baking their specialties for the auction. Students went to the home economics lab to bake pies and cakes and double recipes of cookies and cinnamon buns.

Some drove to their parents' homes and businesses in other states, gathering up items for the auction. Carloads of cheese and bologna and ham arrived from Lancaster. We were caught up in the heat of the fire!

The auction was set for Monday night. Students, faculty, and community people brought their treasures and "laid them at the apostles' feet." Four thousand bodies jammed into the gym. Someone stayed by the thermometer, marking each rise in "temperature," and at every thousand-dollar increase, a bell rang out.

At two o'clock in the morning the thermometer went over the top. Victory! The library would be a reality.

Nothing can stop a Spirit-driven sea of flames! The next morning the local paper's headline screamed, "STUDENTS SET CAMPUS AFIRE!" What a memorable week. I went to Jess's and had a hotdog. Life was good.

> *Acts 2:2.* There came a sound like the rush of a violent wind, and it filled the entire house where they were sitting. Tongues of fire rested on each of them. All of them were filled with the Holy Spirit.

14

Beautiful Blemishes

*The pottery piece shouldn't be half price—
it had "character!"*

We thought we had found the perfect answer to our wedding-gift dilemma.

It seemed to us that I had become a "marrying parson." I had performed close to one hundred fifty marriages and more were scheduled for the coming summer. I almost always brought a gift to the reception. Some said I didn't have to, but I wanted to be more than a marrying professional.

During our ten years at this Pennsylvania church, we had fallen in love with the work of a local potter. His pots and vases and bowls were seen at the large craft shows in the Philadelphia area. His art brought a good price, but we continued to buy it because it made unique and memorable wedding gifts.

Sometimes we would purchase six or seven pieces at a time, so we would be ready for several months of weddings. One afternoon, after we had made our selections from his new stock, we noticed that on the bottom shelf were a number of pieces marked down fifty percent. We examined the pottery and found a large piece we liked just as well as the "top shelf" pieces.

I added this large urn to those already chosen and said to the potter, "I like this piece, I even like the blemish that makes this piece unique." He must have agreed with me, because he decided right then that it shouldn't be half price after all; it had "character."

I learned then and there to keep my mouth shut! It is a costly thing to talk too much. I decided it is much better to be a listener and to allow the potter to describe his own work. Anyhow, we kept on buying the potter's pieces as long as we lived in the area. We thought he made wonderful wedding gifts.

Jeremiah 18:1-4. God told Jeremiah,"Up on your feet! Go to the potter's house. When you get there, I'll tell you what I have to say." So I went to the potter's house, and sure enough, the potter was there, working away at his wheel. Whenever the pot turned out badly, as sometimes happens when you are working with clay, the potter would simply start over and use the same clay to make another pot. (*The Message*)

15

A Shoemaker's Sense of Justice

He forgave Bill, kept him as manager, and let him repay what he stole.

The secretary stood in the office doorway. She said, "There's someone here to see you, and Ura is on the phone!"

I picked up the phone to hear Ura say, "We've found the thief, and it's our own shop foreman! I'm sending him to the church. Can you see him right away?"

I had known for months that Ura's business, the Badorf Shoe Company, was experiencing loss of inventory almost weekly. Somebody was stealing shoes. Not just a few shoes but truckloads of shoes. Ura's sons had been watching the building at night and had informed the Lititz police so they too could be on the lookout.

Ura was a founder of the Akron Mennonite Church, where I was pastor. When we first accepted the call to serve this church, we believed it was largely composed of Mennonite Central Committee people, those radically interested in peace, justice, and simple living. We soon discovered the congregation also had academics, big business owners, and the "rich and famous" jet-set types as well as the peace and justice folks.

In this faith community of liberal and moderate believers, Ura stood out as an arch conservative. He had grown up in the Amish community. Although he later joined the Mennonite church, he had maintained the values learned in his youth. His whole thought process was out of step with many of the other church members.

Ura and his wife Gladys had built a business of making children's leather shoes. They had a retail store where they sold these shoes. Ura was proud of his successful business and employees. He provided employment for dozens of community residents as well as his own sons. The company was thriving. This recent development had him baffled.

Now the mystery was solved, I thought. They would have the culprit arrested and of course, fired on the spot. Wrong! Here was Ura on the phone explaining, "Truman, I am sending Bill over to the church. Can you hear his confession and pray with him?"

Bill was in the outer office, shaking like a leaf. He had been caught in the act. Apparently he had been taking a truckload of shoes every month to a flea market in another county.

I wondered what was going on in his mind now, finding himself in church instead of at the police station!

Bill was to be forgiven, kept on as shop foreman, and given the chance to repay what he had stolen. No hint of anger, malice, or retaliation. For Ura, everything was redeemable. He was a man like no other!

16

A Healing Song

How an hour of daily singing
prevented depression.

Our church was spending the weekend at Spruce Lake Camp in the Poconos, enjoying our annual church retreat. About 7:30 a.m., thinking I had another half hour for sleep, I heard singing in the room next to ours.

Was there a meeting I was supposed to attend? Was I late for the morning service? As I came awake, I remembered that John Landes was in the adjoining room. Then I remembered what he had told me just a few weeks earlier. He had explained, "Singing lifts my spirits."

John was a man of such integrity. Now at age ninety, he lived in a retirement home and had plenty of time to remember a rich and rewarding life. He had married well and raised a family of beautiful children. Often when we sat together, he told me stories of his wife and children.

Not all of his memories were pleasant. Early in his career he found himself at odds with the church. The church had a rule against life insurance—and John sold life insurance.

There was a rule against "special music" and John was a member of a talented men's quartet. John had to be disciplined by the church. Thinking back over these differences with church leaders, John could have been bitter. But he had long ago forgiven the church for having too many rules. He was at peace.

It was when his beautiful wife died at age seventy-two that John had a difficult time. He grieved and longed for his lovely Hannah. It was easy to slip into depression. Sadness seeped into his activities, and it was hard for him to think positive thoughts. How could he ever recover from losing the joy of his life? He saw his family doctor, who was able to recommend medication, but nothing seemed to lift his spirits.

On his own, John discovered a "cure" for his depression. Every morning, to face the day, he would sing through the hymnal: "Amazing Grace," "Count Your Blessings," "What a Friend we have in Jesus," "My Faith Looks Up to Thee," "When I Survey the Wondrous Cross," "Joy to the World."

An hour of singing to prevent depression—it was a new thought for me, but it seemed to make sense. And it worked for John. He could face the day with a song in his heart. He was a contagious man! Instead of spreading gloom, he "released a song."

> *Ephesians 5:19-20.* As you sing psalms and hymns and spiritual songs among yourselves, singing and making melody to the Lord in your hearts, giving thanks to God the Father at all times and for everything in the name of our Lord Jesus Christ.

17

Super Grocer

*"Didn't we shoot hoops together
here years ago?"*

Dave was a sharp businessman. He followed his father in
the grocery business and after his father's death grew the
family business into a fine supermarket. We found it the best in
the area, and we did our shopping there. Dave and Carolyn
were solid members at Blooming Glen.

Dave would sometimes refer to himself as a "banana sales-
man." He told a story that was funny now but not when it was
happening. Dave had a pastor who was concerned about polit-
ical justice. He would preach sermons about the poor people in
the Banana Republic who were not getting paid decent wages
for their produce. The pastor would even suggest that the congregation might boycott the banana trade.

One day, Dave got up the nerve to explain to the pastor,
"You are always telling us about the poor banana growers. You
know, I get a dreadful headache on Sundays. In fact, I am now
on medication for depression."

To Dave's great surprise, the pastor confided, "I'm on medication too!"

This honest exchange between two men, both in kingdom
business, led to the formation of the "Round Table," a group

that still meets biweekly at the local diner. Business persons and pastors eat together and talk about concerns, church, work, and community. Understanding, mutual support, and respect are the "fruits" of this project.

At Round Table we listened to each other's stories—some troublesome, some hilarious. One day Dave had this story to share with the group: Always interested in providing better service to the community, David had set up centers in the grocery aisles where samples were offered to customers. Especially he liked to show off samples from the market's home-bakery.

But in the aisles that were usually meticulously clean, Dave started noticing trails of crumbs leading from the table of baked goods. Employees reported to Dave that a local resident often came to load up on the free samples. He would not take a napkin but would scoop up the cake in his hands and eat it on his way out of the store.

One day Dave saw the trail of crumbs, and he stooped over, picking up crumbs and walking toward the man. He asked the visitor, "Didn't we used to shoot hoops together? How would you like to come out back and shoot some hoops?"

Dave had basketball goals in the warehouse at the rear of the store where off-duty workers could exercise. The two men, the owner and the "problem visitor," shot hoops like old times. What a lesson for all of us—how to confront a problem and how to turn an "enemy" into a friend. Praise the Lord!

18

Albert's A La Carte

*His sandwiches
included alfalfa sprouts and tofu.*

Al had a dream. He was intrigued by the sandwich carts parked each noon in the town square in downtown Lancaster. He already knew what he would someday call his portable business. He would call it A La Carte and would sell only healthy fare.

His sandwiches would include alfalfa sprouts and tofu. His drinks would be fruit juices. His prices would be affordable so the average person could eat lunch at his cart. Finally his special-order operation was ready, and Al opened for business.

I often drove to center city Lancaster to buy lunch at Al's A La Carte. I would buy a sandwich, then look for any place to perch, usually ending up sitting on the curb, watching Al and all the other cart-owners filling orders for the lunch crowd.

This particular day a young man, noticeably a foreigner, came and sat on the curb beside me. We chatted a bit, then he said to me, pointing toward Al, "I would give anything to be like that man." For Al, serving health food and selling it for a little less than cost was the essence of Christian service; somehow this young man had caught the spirit of what Al was all about.

Albert Miller marched to a different drummer. He was the son of a wealthy and well-known shoe merchant from Akron, Pennsylvania. His father was the founder of Mennonite Central Committee (MCC), an agency formed to feed the hungry of the world. Al, like his father, was not interested in becoming a rich man. He wanted to help the down-and-out. He loved to give money away.

Al and his wife did not feel the same way about the use of money. Esther was a gentle, refined, loving person, a hard-working school teacher. She too wanted to be generous with others, but she was realistic about the needs of her household. Al gave money until there was none left to give, then he would approach Esther and try to get her to join his causes. Sometimes I was called upon to act as mediator.

Al suffered a stroke that caused severe limitations. He was in therapy for months. Esther tells about an incident which shows how Al kept his priorities right to the end:

The therapist was doing a reality check.

The therapist held up a pen; Al said, "Write."

He held up his watch; Al said, "Time."

He held up a dollar bill and Al responded, "Give it away."

The therapist was puzzled, thinking that Al might not be as alert as he had hoped. But Esther said, "This is a good sign! Al is getting back to normal. Al believes money is to be given away!"

19

Don Directs *Godspell*

We were glad we had not let
our pastor fears slow him down.

Don was finishing his first year at Hesston College in Kansas. The studies had been challenging and he struggled with some of his classes. But in his areas of interest, he was bigger than life in the things he tackled. He seemed to major in sports, drama, music, and social life. He was having a great year.

As year-end approached, Don began sending messages that he would like to direct a play at church during the summer months. He wanted his mom to write to New York for the rights to perform *Godspell* in our church.

Even before arriving for the summer, Don contacted Akron young people and lined up the cast. His sister Kathleen agreed to be Mary Magdalene, Charles Peachey would play Jesus, Jan Brubaker would be John the Baptist, and Chris Hostetler had a major role. Our future son-in-law, Dean Isaacs, was in charge of promotion.

Play practice filled every evening, often stretching into the night. We started hearing complaints from parents of the younger actors. We heard Don patiently explain that we were limited in time here, the show was scheduled for the first weekend in August, and that practice could not stop at 9:00 p.m. as parents were requesting.

Don's mother and I tried to be boosters from the beginning. Our family had seen the show on Broadway and knew that the message was positive and the young people would benefit from learning the lyrics of this classic. We also knew there were raucous sections, and that we might experience criticism from church members.

We could have relaxed on that front. On the evening of the production, the church was jammed with enthusiastic supporters: parents, grandparents, friends, neighbors, members, and non-members came to enjoy *Godspell.*

Ura Gingrich, whose roots were in the Amish tradition, and his lovely wife Gladys, had front-row seats. A moment stands out in my memory. Kathleen, singing the lusty "Turn Back, Oh Man, Forsake Thy Foolish Ways," danced across the front of the sanctuary, paused beside Ura, and perched on his lap as she sang.

What a proud accomplishment for Don and his troupe. In producing this musical, he had pulled together a most wonderful summer for himself and his peers.

I was glad we had not let our fears slow him down.

Sometimes we learn to say, "O well" and just let things happen. I learned that summer that our son was motivated in ways that I could never be.

Godspell ran a second night and will long be remembered as a high in my life as a father and a pastor.

As we look back on the many wonderful experiences with the lively and progressive members of Akron Church, this stands out as a peak moment.

Mark 14:6. Jesus said, "Let her alone. . . . She has performed a good service for me. . . .Wherever the good news is proclaimed in the whole world, what she has done will be told in remembrance of her.

20

Miracle at Penn State

"Coach, would it be okay if we prayed?"

Every Sunday that September I would ask Randy and Sylvia how Lucas was doing at Penn State. Lucas was one of the horde of students who had left for college that fall. We had a special interest in his well-being. His parents had been so helpful when we first moved to Pennsylvania. In fact, Randy and his younger son, Jason, had driven the big semi that moved our household furnishings from Virginia.

There was another reason we had a special interest in Lucas' entry into college. Randy had called the last Sunday in August and asked if Betty and I could come to their home for a special prayer for Lucas before his departure.

We had formed a circle under a huge oak tree in the yard. Lucas' parents and younger brother gave words of blessing, and Lucas offered love and appreciation for his family. Arms around each other, we prayed for Lucas and his new Penn State life.

Lucas was a world-class swimmer. For years he had trained daily at an Olympic-size pool near Philadelphia. This training paid off when he received a scholarship to Penn State and would be on the university's swim team.

Several weeks passed, and things seemed to be going very well. Then one night Randy and Sylvia got a late-night telephone call. The coach was on the phone telling them this story:

Two students—a girl from the women's team and a boy on the men's team—had been dating. One night they made a terrible decision. They planned a double suicide. Not successful, they were taken to the hospital and would recover. The coach pulled the two teams together to share the awful news.

Of course the teams were devastated. How could their classmates be in such agony and the others were not aware? How could they go on? They were a silent, dejected group.

The coach wanted to share with the Shellys what happened next. Lucas spoke up. "Coach, would it be okay if we prayed?" Coach gave permission and Lucas led in prayer. There was healing and a new sense of togetherness. The team would be able to get back to work and keep their schedule. The coach just wanted to thank godly parents for bringing up a son like Lucas.

Proverbs 22:6. Train children in the right way, and when old, they will not stray.

21

From Mourning to Dancing

*Forgiven, healed, and hopeful
about the future, Sylvia was singing!*

Sylvia's marriage was over. It had been over for years and years, but Sylvia was the last to admit the reality. It had been five years since she discovered her partner's unfaithfulness, but Sylvia still clung to a glimmer of hope that a miracle would bring them back together.

Sylvia is a beautiful person, a gifted counselor and near-professional singer. She had married her college sweetheart, and the two had lovely children, now in their teens. More than anything, Sylvia wanted to salvage her marriage. She was willing to seek counseling, forgive, make changes, anything that would give them another chance.

Her friends and supporters were concerned. They watched her withdraw and fade. She lost her beautiful singing voice. It seemed to her friends that Sylvia was obsessed with recovering her relationship. They tried to convince her that it was time to accept the death of the marriage, and to get on with her life.

One Sunday evening, Sylvia called to talk about her grief. She asked how I would feel about helping to plan a service of

closure for her marriage. She wanted to invite her closest
friends, and she would like to have Scriptures, meditation,
psalms of lament, prayers, silence, a period of waiting, and
singing. Together we worked on a service that could open the
way for forgiveness and healing and hope.

Her friends gathered in the church sanctuary on a Sunday
evening. Following the brief meditation with its theme of "A
New Beginning," many friends responded with prayers and
words of affirmation and encouragement for Sylvia. Then it
was time for Ken to lead us in the song, "My Life Flows On."
We sang the first stanza quietly, then hummed the next stanza,
and still quietly humming, we became aware of a beautiful an-
gelic soprano voice singing:

*What though my joys and comforts die? The Lord my Savior
  liveth,*
*What though the darkness gather round? Songs in the night he
  giveth.*

Sylvia was singing! After years of not being able to sing, she
had found her voice! After her "dark night of the soul," forgiven, healed, hopeful about the future, Sylvia was singing! At
the end of the verse, we all joined in.

*No storm can shake my inmost calm while to that Rock I'm
  clinging.*
*Since love is Lord of heaven and earth, how can I keep from
  singing?*

Psalm 30: 11-12. You turned my mourning into dancing; you removed my sackcloth and clothed me with joy,
that my heart may sing to you and not be silent. O Lord
my God, I will give you thanks forever.

22

The Father's Care

*Marion had the distinct feeling
that she had been visited by God.*

O ur friend Marion was facing serious surgery. How could she think about anything else? And how could she wait for two weeks, with this hanging over her head?

As was her custom, she walked with Mel to his pickup that morning and kissed him good-bye. As she slowly returned to the house, she noticed a single beautiful rose blooming beside the gatepost, and a blue jay perched nearby. She turned to wave again to her husband, then walked into the house. Just outside her kitchen window sat that same blue jay! She could tell the bird wanted to come in, so she opened the window. The bird fluttered in and settled on the kitchen counter. It took a few pecks at the diced vegetables on the chopping board, then turned and flew back out the window.

Marion had the distinct feeling that she had been visited by God. Just when she desperately needed a message, God came to her in this surprising way. This was not the only visitation she experienced in the coming week. She describes the next occurrence.

Marion and Mel decided to drive to Chesapeake that Sunday where Cousin Robert (Bobby) Mast was scheduled to preach. It was an hour-long drive, and Marion opened her Bible to read aloud the passage from Matthew 6:25-26. The passage seemed to be a direct message from God:

> Therefore, I tell you, do not be anxious for your life, what you shall eat and what you shall drink, nor about your body, what you shall put on. Is not life more than food? And the body more than clothing? Look at the birds of the air . . . they neither sow nor reap, nor gather into barns, and your heavenly Father feeds them. Are you not worth more than the birds?

Imagine her surprise when they arrived at church and heard Bob announce his text from Matthew 6: "Therefore, I tell you, do not be anxious about your life." Beyond any shadow of doubt, Marion got the message. Through "the birds of the field," through her own reading of Scripture, and now through the sermon from Matthew, she gleaned messages of reassurance from a loving heavenly Father.

Were these coincidences that happened for Marion? I believe that miracles abound on every side. When we are looking, when we are tuned in, God is there! Amen.

23

Soaring Home

*During a final hymn, cages were opened
and pigeons exploded upward.*

Jesse and Rachel returned to Blooming Glen after forty years
of living and working in New Jersey. They had been among
the lay supporters who helped the pastor couple plant Alpha
Mennonite Church.

Now back at the home church, in retirement, they made
such a rich contribution to all of us. Rachel was an avid reader
and helped to enrich our church library. Jesse restored an old
Model A pickup until it was better than new and would bring it
to church weddings to give the bride and groom a ceremonial
ride.

Another hobby of Jesse's was his homing pigeons. But
when the couple moved into a retirement home, he had to let
his neighbor take over this hobby. Rachel and Jesse celebrated
life in retirement. I was often invited into their home for deli-
cious home-cooked meals.

The time came when Jesse was called home to be with the
Lord. His funeral service was thoughtful and inspiring; he had
planned the service, and it reflected a life lived well. After the
service indoors, we crossed the road for graveside prayers and a
service of committal.

At the appointed time, during a final hymn,
    the pigeon cage was opened,
        the birds exploded from their confinement.
       Up, up, up,
          they wheeled in large circles,
            soaring high into the wide,
              expansive sky,
                then finally circling back.
With high, piercing cries, they zoomed straight for home.
What a picture!
What a symbol!

Jesse had gone home and we were left standing, our faces lifted in wonder and amazement as we watched. It seemed as if we had seen his soul soaring toward his eternal home. Jesse had made his home-going a gift to us all, with an invitation to consider our own soul's yearning for home.

And I Will Raise You Up

*And I will raise you up on eagle's wings, bear you on the breath of
    dawn,
Make you to shine like the sun, and hold you in the palm of my
    hand.*
——Based on Psalm 91

24

A House Built from Scraps

After I calmed down, we took movies of the children's accomplishment.

I came driving in the lane of our new home and behold, I saw a new structure that had not been there this morning! On top of the structure stood Steve, busily tacking on the roof, and Kathy and Don handing him more shingles and more nails. All three paused to wave a welcome.

My first impulse was to protest. My neat stacks of lumber, the boxes of left-over tile, pieces of sheet-rock, nails—all hauled out of the garage and nailed together in this shack leaning against the front of the house.

But I had been forewarned, and I was trying to keep my mouth shut. Betty had called me at the office, and the way she explained it, the children had been happily occupied all day, not even wanting to take time for lunch. She had carried their lunch out to the work-place. And she herself had enjoyed the most wonderful day, with three children excited about their project. It was a learning experience for them!

We had just moved into our new house on Hillcrest Avenue. It was our aim to be in before school started, and we had accomplished the goal. Lots of family members and friends had pitched in to get the project completed. My brother-in-law, Nevin Steiner, and his four brothers had come for a week in June to frame the structure. Other subcontractors had reworked their summer schedules to accommodate us.

A lot of small projects still needed my attention. Along one inside wall of the garage I had neatly stacked all the left-over material I could use for ongoing projects—short pieces of lumber, tile, roofing, nails, sheet-rock.

This last week of summer was special because nephew Steve came to spend the week with Kathy and Don. It was a week of adventure and fun, with Steve, age nine, leading and directing many of the activities. We took lots of movies of the three cousins.

After I calmed down and could bring myself to inspect the house and congratulate the builders on their fine work, we got out the camera and took movies of this major accomplishment.

The house stood there for a number of weeks, a proud memorial to the ingenuity and aptitude of the builders.

Some weeks later I took the house down. It had served its purpose. I pulled out the crooked and bent nails, stacked the lumber against the wall of the garage, boxed up the shingles and tiles. A Bible verse took on new meaning, "When I became a man, I put away childish things."

Recently when we asked Steve if he remembered this particular project, he laughed. Of course he remembered.

When he came to visit us that summer, he had just completed his own building project—a tree house in his granddad's backyard. He felt like an experienced builder, and when he saw all the good lumber and building materials stacked, ready and waiting, he just couldn't resist.

25

Christmas Is a Love Story (Sermon)

"Turn off the motor, wait, listen for the snow bells ringing."

Do we need a soul-enlargement this Advent Season?

Our souls seem to have shriveled,
Unlike Joseph and Mary,
Simeon and Anna,
The shepherds,
The wise men.

Do we magnify the Lord, as did Mary in the Magnificat?
Our appetite for the transcendent is small.
We prefer to keep our mysteries contained.
Our harps are hardly tuned.

I catch myself hungry, longing for the mystery,
the delight, the poetry I once knew as a child.
Some persons do keep their harps tuned.
Breezes of grace caress the strings,
And there is soul music.

I remember the words of Gertrude in Akron, Pennsylvania.
It was January.
Snow covered the ground.
"Truman," she instructed me. "Go down the road, park by the old
mansion.
Turn off your motor. Roll down the window.
Wait, wait, wait.
Quiet, quiet, quiet.
Listen, listen, listen.
You will hear snow bells, ringing in the spring."
What was she telling me?

There's music playing in the universe. The whole earth is full of
the glory of God! And most of us are not hearing the music! As
Phillips Brooks wrote,

How silently, how silently, the wondrous gift is given,
So God imparts to human hearts the blessings of the heav'ns.
No ear may hear his coming, but in this world of sin,
Where meek souls will receive him still the dear Christ enters in.

We need to have our hearts tuned to receive the message.
  It is possible to miss it completely.
    To have heard nothing!
He came to his own and they didn't know him, nor did they re-
ceive him.

Once when I traveled in Rome, I saw an instrument hanging
on an outside wall. It was the famous Aeoleon Harp, so deli-
cately strung that, when tuned just right, at the slightest breeze
it begins to play. Isn't this an image of God's grace, playing im-
perceptibly on the sounding board of the human heart!
  An ancient poet wrote,

Thou shalt know him when he comes,
Not by any din of drums,
Nor by the vantage of his airs,
Not by anything he wears.

Neither by his gown, nor his crown,
For his presence shall be known by the Holy Harmony
that his coming works in thee.

Fine music, delicate melody. As contrasted to Old Testament
thundering and lightning and earthshaking preceding God's
dramatic revelations and entrance.
Drums, brass, trumpets then.

Now we listen in the gaps waiting for a glimpse.
We listen with ear cocked for his sign.
We tune our hearts for the long awaited message.
Like John the Baptist of old, we wait in our prisons.
Is he the one who is to come, or do we look for another?

Great is the mystery of godliness!
We want God strong.
> *He wants to be weak!*
> *He became a baby!*
> *Amazing message of all time!*
> *He came to his own hidden, unrecognized, incognito,*
> *The world could not recognize him, they passed him by.*

John the Baptist pointed, "There he is!"
Only a scant few believed.

Why would God disclose himself hidden? So hidden that people could miss him? Why the mysterious? Kierkegaard, en-
dowed with rich imagination, told his own parable.

Once upon a time there was a king,
> *Regal, handsome, strong, loved and respected by all.*
> *He ruled a vast country.*
He fell in love with a peasant girl of humble origin living in a
hovel.
The king assembled his wise persons and asked their advice
on how to declare his love.
The wise persons said, "Your majesty, appear in all your glory
before her humble abode and instantly
she will fall on her knees and be yours."

But that was precisely what was disturbing the king.
He did not want his own glorification.
  He wanted her glorification.
    In return for his love, he wanted her love.
Night after night he walked the floor of the palace.
Not to declare his love meant the death of love,
  and to declare it was the death of his beloved.
He paced back and forth, pondering, lonesome, sad, and per-
    plexed.
Finally the king saw a truth:
  Freedom for the beloved demands equality with the beloved.
Late one night after all his wise persons had retired,
  he dressed in servant clothes,
    well worn and tattered.
Down the street he strode, through the countryside,
  to the door of the shanty where she lived.

A lovely story? Instinctively, we want to know more. We want to ask questions. Investigate. The storyteller knew well that if

God loves every maiden, every man, every baby, every child,
  then he approaches us with love clothed in humility,
    the garb and flesh of us all.

And it follows that we can respond to that love with a surrender of
  our own!
This advent he approaches our hovels, our homes,
  Clothed in flesh, the flesh of a child.
What can bring us to our knees more quickly than a child?
  What can bring a tear to our eyes more rapidly than a child?
    What can cause us to whisper and show love more easily
      than a child?
      What is more disarming than a child?
When the king comes to the cottage door,
So silently, so hidden, so unobtrusive,
I hope the maiden opens the door and returns his love.
And I hope when Jesus, clothed in humanity,

knocks at our door this season, we open the door.
For the face that looks at us out of eternity is a human face, dressed
*   as a servant.*

He has spent hours pacing the palace floor,
And finally out of the side door of heaven,
*   Down through the passages of time,*
*   Into a crude stable stall,*
*   Passionately in love with us,*
*   Without destroying our humanity but instead fulfilling our*
*   humanity,*
*   He comes.*

I look to him and I see what I was designed to be!
He whispers peace.
"Peace with God and peace with your fellow human beings."
More than anything this Christmas we feel the longing and the
*   tuning of our heart strings.*
*   Silently tuned.*
*   Tuned to hear the breeze of grace playing at Mary's heart.*
*   Playing at our hearts.*
Tuned for the amazing, magical miracle of a love story.

"How silently, how silently the wondrous gift is given. . . ."
I remember hearing the story of the author of these lines.
Phillips Brooks was one of the outstanding preachers in this
country in the 1800's. But he entered a period of depression
and felt a need for rest and a complete change of scenery. He
journeyed to the Holy Land in hopes of recovery and inspiration. Christmas Eve found him in a field overlooking Bethlehem. Feeling inspired by the sight of the little holy town at
twilight, Brooks took out his tablet and penned these words:

O little town of Bethlehem,
How still we see thee lie;
Above thy deep and dreamless sleep
The silent stars go by;
Yet in thy dark streets shineth

The everlasting light.
The hopes and fears of all the years
Are met in thee tonight.

O holy Child of Bethlehem,
Descend to us, we pray;
Cast out our sin and enter in,
Be born in us today.
We hear the Christmas angels
The great glad tidings tell,
O come to us, abide with us,
Out Lord Emmanuel !

Brooks returned home, the depression lifted. He entered the pulpit and preached with a holy fervor. He had been to the Promised Land!

Part 2

CAP'N JACK

*Stories of
Salvation and Grace*

Part 2

Introduction

I have been keenly aware of those in church settings who are excluded or left out or never quite make the inner circle. I have attempted through pastoral work and preaching to be welcoming and inclusive, believing that God's arms are open to those who have been rejected.

I believe in the powerful grace of God at work in the world—welcoming the excluded, the down and out, the needy, and the marginal people. It is a mystery to me that Christians who claim to believe every word of Scripture still find it possible to be exclusive and rejecting of those Christ says he came to save.

In the balance between grace and judgment, I would rather err on the side of grace. I might be considered by some of my spiritual brothers and sisters to be too open in welcoming, especially in areas that have become toxic issues for the church.

From my earliest pastorate in the 1970s, I was persistent in my request to have women share the platform. Planning committees knew that I would like to have a woman read Scripture or lead singing or tell the children's story. This was a small step in the days when our churches were rejecting women in leadership roles. This sometimes put me at odds with the planning committees, even the women on the committees, many of whom were satisfied with the status quo.

In the last couple of years, our church has adopted the slogan, "Across the Street and Around the World." To me this emphasizes our desire to be hospitable as well as mission-minded. Our church is learning to communicate a message of welcome. This has been my desire: to reach out with open arms to those seeking a home and to use words of welcome in every situation.

The story of Cap'n Jack is about one outside the walls. I am thankful that Uncle Henry reached out to him, cared for him, and brought him inside the doors of our church. And I am thankful that the church family responded, "Naturally, come on in."

1

A Priest at Every Elbow (Sermon)

Miracle of miracles,
Cap'n Jack asked to be baptized.

I grew up in the Colony. It was a Paradise, a walled garden. A hundred years before my time, pioneers traveled to southern Virginia from Ohio, in search of good farmland. They found an old, run-down plantation with several thousand acres, bought it and divided it into small farms.

It was truly a walled garden of dairies, peach and apple orchards, truck patches, and chicken houses. We all knew exactly where the Colony started and where it ended.

Just beyond the walls of our paradise lived Cap'n Jack. An old seafaring captain, he made his living as an oyster-man.

We children were deadly afraid of Cap'n Jack. We had heard stories about him and his drinking. When he would come staggering through the Colony we would run into the house and hide under the table.

Uncle Henry was a devout man in our Colony. He was the exact opposite of Cap'n Jack in every way. He was meticulous and careful about his appearance, almost a perfectionist in his manner of living.

One day God said to Uncle Henry, "Go down to the river and join Cap'n Jack. Pray for him, go sit with him." For twenty years, every Sunday afternoon, while the rest of us were snoozing or reading or playing, Uncle Henry went to spend the afternoon with Cap'n Jack and his cats. They would sometimes eat together, using plates that the cats had licked clean.

I remember the Sunday when the door of the church opened wide, and in walked Uncle Henry with Cap'n Jack on his arm. They came together the next Sunday and the next. Then, miracle of miracles, Cap'n Jack asked to be baptized.

My father had the privilege of performing the baptism, pouring the water over his head and saying, "Arise! I give you my hand, and even as Christ was raised from the dead, you, too, shall walk in newness of life."

Now when I go back to the Colony, I walk through the cemetery across from the church where all the saints are buried. I look for the marker that is engraved, "Captain Jack Watson, 1865-1953."

In Acts 8 we read about the spread of the gospel beyond the walls of Judaism.

One day God said to Philip,
"Go south to the road,
the desert road,
that goes down from Jerusalem to Gaza.
Go join yourself and stay near that chariot."
So he started out.

It was about noon.
You don't go to the desert at noon!
That's not a good idea!
You will get "fried."

But Philip obeyed and went
To the desert alone.

Frequently we are called to leave our comfortable,
  rewarding, walled-in garden,
and we find ourselves in a hard place.
  Alone and barren.

It was there that Philip met the Ethiopian eunuch.
  The eunuch created a dilemma for Philip on three fronts:
1. He was a foreigner. Every Israelite kept his distance from for-
    eigners.
      You just didn't get close to them.
      You kept your distance to keep clean!

2. He was a eunuch. Eunuchs were damaged.
  Sexually damaged people, not allowed within the covenant
    community.
      Banned from the temple courts.
      To be kept at arms' length.

3. He was very rich. Now isn't that cause for suspicion?
  Not as bad as being a foreigner or
    sexually damaged,
      But surely a negative!

And into the eunuch's world, into his heart and soul,
  into his famished spirit,
    Came the gospel message:
God loves the foreigner!
    God loves the damaged person, the abused, the destitute!
      God loves rich people!
        God loves! He loves! He loves!

Philip "good-newsed" the eunuch.
  Sweeping grace is offered!
      A message to hurting, damaged people.
        To those uncertain about whether the Lord is
        with them,

Battling feelings of rejection,
Wounded, guilty, sad, hopeless.
Sinking down, down,
Near the end with no way out.

In anguish from the abusive pains of childhood.
Indescribable scars and fears and suffering.

I can never know the deepest pain of your journey,
But I do know this—the Lord loves.
He loves and loves and loves.
A suffering Christ walks beside you.
He whispers, "I love you. Don't give up. Don't give up."

People are brought daily into our lives and God says,
"Go. Leave your walled garden.
Join yourself to them.
Pray with them, Sit with them.
Good-news them with the hope of the gospel!
Love them."

God loves a lot of people I have not yet learned to love!
"O God, help me to look inside and discover,
in the most personal terms,
how Christ has changed/transformed/healed me.
And then, please, God,
Open my eyes, open my heart
to those around me, riding alone.

"Give me urgency, give me compassion, give me love,
help me run, reaching out with your grace,
good-newsing them with your gospel."

2

Barnacles

One day the throttle did not
respond, and we sat dead in the water.

I dreamed of the day when I would have a really good speedboat instead of my little rowboat. Living along the Warwick
River, it seemed almost a necessity that I own a better boat. It
would come in handy for taking friends out fishing or just
spending a few hours on the river after a hard day's work.

Finally the day came. The boat was sleek and powerful. She
could rise up out of the water and skim across the surface at
great speed. I anchored it near our house, down by the creek,
and took every opportunity to run up and down the river, loving the sense of power and speed. This boat exceeded my ex-
pectations! Whoever the boat's crafters were knew what they
were doing.

Our Pennsylvania friends came for the weekend, and one
highlight was to be a boat-ride on the river. Maybe we would go
as far as the James and have a look at the shipyard. We would
give them a fun river experience.

That Saturday was the perfect spring day, sunny and bright
and breezy. Early in the afternoon, the four of us went down to
the creek to board the boat. We headed for the open waters, and
I pushed the throttle forward. No response! No sudden surge of

power! The motor labored harder, but nothing would make it speed up.

I reached my hand below the water-line and it hit me: Barnacles! The hull of my boat was covered with these little clam-like critters. We were not going anywhere fast that day. My dream of an exciting ride was over.

Saul Bellows once defined "safe" religion as a "kitchen religion, having nothing to do with God's great acts in history—just slow, tame, and unexciting." I have observed over the years those new, sincere Christians who take off full speed ahead, then slow down to a snail's pace. The little besetting sins take hold like barnacles and fasten onto our souls. One day the throttle does not respond and we sit dead in the water, in our "trespasses and sins."

As for my speedboat, the professionals reminded me that while my boat was docked, the slow-moving, stagnant waters provided the perfect breeding ground for barnacles. After it was cleaned and scraped, the boat performed as intended. It's the same with all of us. We too need to be cleaned up so that we can get free of the barnacles and critters that keep us bogged down. That is an ongoing part of the redemption story.

Ephesians 2. As for you, you were dead in your transgressions and sins . . . but because of his great love for us, God who is rich in mercy, made us alive with Christ even when we were dead in transgressions.

3

The Launching

The huge ship rose to the surface and floated on her own.

The *S. S. United States* was to be the biggest, fastest, most luxurious passenger ship ever to ply the oceans. She was built in my hometown, at the Newport News Shipbuilding and Dry Dock. Weekly I drove to Newport News to watch the progress of this huge undertaking. I watched the builders lay the giant keel and then, over months and years, watched as ton after ton of steel was added.

From the beginning, the shipbuilders knew that the huge ship would not be launched in the usual manner, sliding down gangplanks into the James River. This ship would be built in a giant holding tank, and when the ship was finished, the holding tank would be filled with water. The ship would rise in the tank and be released into the sea.

Launching day came. Launching was scheduled for twelve noon. Early in the morning, the holding tank was opened to be filled by seawater. I joined the huge crowd that gathered for this historic occasion. The clock struck twelve. There was silence as we held our breath and watched.

Then, miracle of miracles, the huge vessel tilted as she floated to the surface. The roar of the crowd was deafening.

What high excitement! What a thrilling moment, never to be forgotten.

That momentous day is still vivid in my memory. When I think of the moment the big ship rose to the surface and floated on her own, I think of the story of Pentecost. The church was in dry dock, awaiting the coming of the Holy Spirit. A huge crowd was gathered. Listen to the story

> *Acts 2:1-4.* When the day of Pentecost had come, they were all together in one place. And suddenly from heaven there came a sound like the rush of a violent wind, and it filled the entire house where they were sitting. Divided tongues, as of fire, appeared among them, and a tongue rested on each of them. All were filled with the Holy Spirit.

I was at the launching of the *S. S. United States.* That human-made wonder is now in mothballs and retired. I have been to Pentecost! This God-made wonder is more active than ever, filling God's people with God's love and power.

4

Miracles
Begin at Home

The billfold was somewhere in the orchard,
probably plowed under.

I remember Dad standing in the open doorway, leaning his large body against the frame, and saying, "Mother, in our lifetime we will never be out of debt." It was the 1930s, and our family had moved back to the Colony from Washington, D.C., where Dad was a successful building contractor. Successful to a fault! When the Depression hit, owners simply moved out and the houses were back in Dad's name.

Bankruptcy would have been an expected path to take (as his customers had done), but Dad felt a moral obligation to pay back every cent he owed the banks. I heard Dad explain, "I tried to sell these houses, but there was simply no market. Nobody had money."

Starting over, my parents planted peach and apple orchards and prayed for better days. They dreamed of once again being successful. They hoped at least to be able to pay off their huge loans in Washington, D.C.

It was hard to keep a positive spirit. We were a poor family, and we knew it. Our house was covered with tar-paper waiting for the day we could afford siding. We had food from our own garden but no money for buying extras.

In early spring Dad would go to the bank and borrow enough money to spray the trees and prepare the orchard for the coming season. This money was supposed to last until the first peaches were ripe and there would be income again.

On this particular Monday morning, Dad made his annual borrowing trip to the bank and received $300 in cash. Then he proceeded to the orchard, where he disked and plowed all day long. When he came in for supper, he reached for his billfold—it was gone! With a look of despair on his face, it dawned on him that the billfold was somewhere in that twenty-five-acre orchard, probably plowed under.

I was only eight, but I knew calamity when I saw it. I realized that $300 was a huge amount of money. I knew Dad was still paying off debts and that we desperately needed a good fruit harvest.

My mother seemed to have a special prayer connection. She passed that strong faith along to her children. So it was only natural that I should pray about this emergency. I slipped upstairs, knelt by my bed, and poured out my earnest plea.

I received this distinct reassurance: "Go with Dad to the orchard, and you will find the billfold."

It took a little convincing, since it was already dark. But Dad agreed to go. He held his large flashlight, pointing the beam out ahead. We tramped through the orchard, Dad taking huge steps, following the path of the tractor through the plowed ground, with me lurching along behind.

I stumbled and fell hard to the ground. The beam of the flashlight caught the billfold flying up into the air. In my fall I had kicked it out of the ground!

Dad and I celebrated. It was a miracle! We hurried to the house to celebrate with Mom. We thanked our heavenly Father. For an eight-year-old boy, it was a huge answer to prayer, and one more building block of faith.

Then came 1947, the year of our turnaround. The orchard yielded a bumper crop. Load after load of peaches was hauled from the orchard to Williamsburg and Yorktown, Newport News, and Norfolk, even to Richmond. People had money again. They could buy our peaches! Money flowed in. Dad carefully counted the money and placed it in a large suitcase.

When September came and we had sold the last peach, the suitcase was jammed. Dad said to Mom, "Let's go to the bank. We have enough."

The three of us drove to the Bank of Warwick, Mom in the front of the truck with Dad. I rode in the back of the truck, elated to have parents who could finally celebrate. It was a day none of us ever forgot!

In the days following, Dad bought candy bars. Not just a few, but whole boxes from the wholesale place. He would buy a case of cookies and bring them home as a surprise. He bought a new car. It was celebration time!

5

Dad Was a Balcony Person

He walked to my desk, picked up a pen,
and wrote on my new blotter!

I learned early in my ministry that every church has two kinds of people: basement dwellers and balcony people.
Basement people do all they can to pull you down.
They grumble,
They moan and groan,
They're always unhappy
And want you to be unhappy too.
Balcony people are the opposite: they do all they can to build you up!
If they sense you are down they will say:
Go for it!
You can do it!
Shouts of encouragement,
Praise and blessing.

My dad sat in the balcony of my life. He was always giving encouragement and praise. For years he had requested a tape of the Sunday services and would listen to it then phone me. He would say, "You may be the best preacher in the whole United

States right now!" I would take this with a grain of salt, but at the same time I relished his enthusiastic words.

Dad and Mom came to Blooming Glen for my installation service, and Dad was asked to pray a blessing at the close of the service. With his stately bearing he walked to the front of the church and in a strong voice prayed a blessing on my work and on the church. He seemed an elder statesman, and I was proud.

After the service I was eager to show the family my new church office. It was important to me for them to know where I would study and write and be pastor. I had worked hard to get all of the books in order, all the clutter cleared away, a fresh blotter on my desk.

I ushered Dad into the room. He walked straight to the desk and sat in my chair, took up my pen, and wrote on my new blotter! I started to reach out to stop him—I liked the clean new blotter and wanted to keep it that way. But he was my dad and I let him go. I had to pay attention to others coming and going through the office.

When the church was quiet, and all the family had left, I had a chance to see what Dad wrote. It was so precious that when the blotter needed replacing, I tore off and kept the corner that had this message: "God Bless You, My Dear Son."

Even now, I know Dad is in the balcony of heaven shouting out encouragement:

"You can do it! Go for it! Don't give up!"

6

Building Up Joey

He was getting smaller and smaller until finally he was only a dot.

Helen sat across the desk in the church office. She was describing her family's current state of health. They were in crisis mode. At the root of the problem was Joey, age eight, and his dislike for second grade. He hated school! He hated his teacher! He often had a stomachache when the big yellow bus came for him.

I asked Helen if Joey would be available for an office visit, and she thought she could talk him into coming. Joey would be my youngest counselee. When he knocked on the door, he was pretty gloomy and down, but the longer we talked, the more responsive he became. I asked Joey to draw a picture of his classroom.

In his first sketch the Big Big Teacher was standing at Joey's desk, yelling. Then he added a series of pictures of Little Joey, getting smaller and smaller until finally he was only a dot. Joey had indeed been hammered down to nothing.

When Joey left the office that day, he had an assignment. He was to write a description of himself, telling what he could do, naming some of his accomplishments.

On Sunday he handed me the folded page:

Joey can:
Play the guitar,
   Play soccer and skateboard,
    Fish,
     Invent things,
      Has a good imagination
       Believes in God,
        Is loving and generous.

The page was crammed full of what Joey could do. He had not been totally destroyed by his teacher. There was hope for Joey. This whole scene got me to thinking how powerful we are in our relationships. We can use our power to
   Put down,
  Reduce,
  Overwhelm,
 Destroy,
And kill the soul of a child.

But we possess an even greater power, one that will
   Build up,
  Honor and bless,
  Encourage, enrich, and empower,
 And give life to the soul of a child.

I encouraged his family and friends to use their gifts to build up Joey. He grew and grew and became a mighty good person!

Mark 9:42. If any of you put a stumbling block before one of these little ones who believe in me, it would be better for you if a great millstone were hung around your neck and you were thrown into the sea.

yell yell yell yell yell yell yell yell yell yell yell yell yell yell yell yell yell yell yell yell yell yell yell yell yell yell yell yell yell yell yell yell yell yell yell yell yell yell yell yell

She is getting smaller, and smaller, and smaller, and.

7

A Note from Kathleen

"Dear Daddy, It's hard to be a Brunk!"

Our children have had a profound influence on my life and ministry. Daughter Margaret Kathleen and son, Donald Wayne, have been a tremendous blessing and in surprising ways have changed my life.

Once when Kathy was six and just learning to write, I was privileged to be the recipient of her first letter. For some breaking of the rules, she had been sent to her room for time out. At the end of the hour I heard her come quietly down the hallway, to my desk where I was working. She laid a scrap of paper in front of me. I read, "Dear Daddy, It is hard to be a Brunk." I picked her up and held her close.

When Kathy was twelve, the family was celebrating my forty-first birthday. She presented me with another letter:

Dear Daddy,
You will soon have to decide whether you will be
a rugged mountain climber
or a humble priest in the Valley.

Again I held her close. She had touched a tender place. I didn't know yet which I would be. Thirty years later I know: I have been the humble priest in the Valley.

A few years later on another birthday, she collaborated with her mother for a very special gift. I awoke to piano music and knew it was Kathy. She played like no other. She pounded the keys with a firmness that could shake the earth. She had memorized my favorite, "Bridge Over Troubled Water."

Whenever Kathy comes home to visit, she knows her greatest gift will be the times she sits at the piano and fills the house with music. And she still includes that early favorite, "Bridge Over Troubled Water." Even now as I think of this, I take her in my arms and thank God for what a blessing she is to our family

Daughter's Essay About Dad
(A High School Assignment)

I can remember coming up with a poster for my dad's birthday several years ago. It went something like this: "Dad, You've reached the point in your life where you have to decide whether you want to be a humble priest in the valley or go and become a daring mountain climber." Well, he chose the former. That's why I'm writing this.

The earliest thing I remember noticing about my dad's faith was the way our house was always open to visiting preachers for them to stay. And there were also the weekly Bible study sessions with our family. Dad would read the Scripture in such a way that Donnie and I would fight over who got to answer questions he would ask. Since my dad was pastor of students at the college, I always felt I had one up on the other kids because his job was relating to young people.

I really like my dad's style of Christianity. It doesn't say that you have to be a perfect person or a perfect Christian. It's a simple, honest relationship to God, and I can see that. He has always been an encouraging person, even to me about my writing. He asked me to write a piece about him and his dad in the hometown church one Sunday.

Through his love for his parents it has been easier for me to see the kind of love the Bible talks about in regard to your parents and for me to carry it out in my daily life.

Through his growing and changing relationship in marriage with Mom, I can see that it is possible to survive a marriage. I also like the equalness of responsibility and concern for each other's fulfillment that they share.

My dad is not afraid to bring out a different opinion or view. He does it with love and mutual concern rather than an air of reprimanding or authoritativeness. He appreciates individuality, and this is one quality I really admire. He accepts me for who I am and where I am in my spiritual growth and doesn't expect me to be better or worse—but me. I really love him for this, and I can see his love through it.

The most important or impressionable thing for me is that he lives what he believes and speaks about. A prime example of this would be our recent move to the townhouses behind the college. We used to live in a fairly nice house that my dad had built. It was nothing lavish, but we had a hard time making ends meet, trying to pay water and electric bills. A conscientious friend of Dad's would refuse to stay in our house when he came to visit. This brought out some serious concerns about our style of living.

Now a lot of people will just sit there and feel guilty and maybe start giving bigger tithes. But this was not so with our family. It was hard for us to move from so much space to a smaller house. In our new house I feel more of the community and not isolated on a hill. I think I feel more of the brotherly care and love that comes from belonging to such a community.

So in conclusion I would like to say that though my father and I aren't as close as my mother and I, he has been a real spiritual inspiration to me. He lives the kind of Christianity that you would want to become a part of. He has made it real for me instead of something to stand back and look at.

8

Finding a
Wife for Beryl

*Amid the youth hubbub, electricity
sparkled between the two.*

In my eighth year at Akron Mennonite Church, our home
church in Virginia needed a pastor and asked if I would consider the position. By now we had been gone from the Colony
for fifteen years, our four parents were in their eighties, and
Betty urged me to accept this assignment at Warwick River
Church in Newport News, Virginia.

It would not be easy to leave the energetic, thriving Akron
congregation in Pennsylvania. We had learned to know a lot of
these people on a personal basis, and it would mean pulling up
stakes, selling our home, leaving a job Betty loved and starting
over again. There was also the worry about how we would relate
to the many family members back in the Colony. It wouldn't be
like it had been, because now I would be the pastor, and that
could be awkward.

We decided to accept the call, and there was some excitement about returning to the south. We bought a lot near the
river and had a house built. Family members in the building
business did a lot of the carpentry and cabinetry. My own fa-

ther, in his eighties, worked with the various subcontractors. He had a new focus in life—he was ready for his son to return.

We moved in June, I started going to the church office each day, and the work was enjoyable. The little church had a thriving Christian school, and in September when school opened, I learned to know some of the teachers. I particularly noticed a beautiful young woman as she lead the music classes. My thoughts turned to Beryl, the youth pastor back at Akron. I had noticed that Beryl gravitated toward young women who "needed" him, and I hoped to see him with someone who could relate on equal footing.

The more I thought of these two young people, one in Virginia and one in Pennsylvania, the more I began to feel inspired. I would get the two together—it couldn't hurt, and it might lead to something permanent! I called Margo and asked if she'd be interested in helping with music if we had a "Youth lock-in." I explained that it would be the Warwick River youth inviting the Akron youth to come to Virginia. Then I admitted to Margo, "Also, there is a young man named Beryl Jantzi I want you to meet."

Margo laughed and consented to help with the lock-in. Next I placed the call to Pennsylvania: "Beryl, I miss you! Would you be willing to bring the Akron youth group for a lock-in with our Warwick River youth? And, by the way, there is a young woman here named Margo Maust I really want you to meet."

The bus arrived late Friday night. Amid all the hubbub, games, snacks, sleeping bags, and hilarity of a lock-in, Beryl and Margo met. There was electricity. When Sunday noon arrived and it was time to load the bus, the two were nowhere to be found. They were making good use of the final minutes, exchanging phone numbers and even setting a date to meet again.

Beryl moved to the Colony to firm up the relationship. A year later they asked Betty and me to perform the wedding ceremony.

Years later we continue to be in contact with Beryl and Margo and Rose and Melissa.

God moves in miraculous ways his wonders to perform!

Proverbs 18:22. He who finds a wife finds a good thing, and obtains favor from the Lord.

9

The Last Love Letters

"Soon I will be taking a long journey."

Dad went to the hospital in January. He had a cough that wouldn't go away. On the way to Riverside Hospital, he told my sister Evelyn, "Soon I will be taking a long journey."

At ninety-two years of age, he accepted reality and was trying to prepare the family for his departure. He had been the strong one for himself and Mom, but it was becoming apparent that he would probably be the first to leave.

Dad and Mom had been soulmates for a long time—they were married more than seventy years. Mom worked side-by-side with Dad in all areas of their life together. Whether in raising a family, working in the peach orchard, or preparing the Sunday sermon, they were partners. They were wonderful models for their children and grandchildren.

I was living in Pennsylvania, three hundred miles from Dad and Mom when this last illness struck. I made frequent trips to spend time with Dad. When I arrived in the Colony, I stopped at the house and took Mom along with me to the hospital. They wept in each other's arms. It was so heartbreaking. I too was in tears.

Sometimes Mom was not well enough to go with me to the hospital. Then I became a letter-carrier between the two of them. I still have the last letters they wrote to each other. Dad wrote:

My precious dear sweetheart,
I love you
forever and forever.
I do wish with all my heart
that I could be with you.
Dear Sweetheart,
there is no one like you
so precious.
—Truman

And my mother wrote,

To my lover and husband
I loved you way back then
when we were young and carefree.
I loved you through all the years
of our toiling and growing together.
I love you now and I love you forever and forever
—From the one you call Ruthie

Early one Monday in January I made my third trip to visit Dad. Soon after I arrived, the family surrounded his bed. His doctor came into the room with a report from his recent tests. He informed Dad that some cancer was in his lung tissue.

The doctor asked, "Do you want us to begin treatment, or do you want us to make you as comfortable as possible?" Dad responded in the way he had planned long before, "No treatment, just do what you can to make me comfortable."

That evening when I embraced Dad, he said, "You'd better return to Pennsylvania. I am alright." Betty and I left, thinking there would be more visits.

We arrived back home about midnight and had been asleep only a few hours when the phone rang. It was Evelyn, "Dad just left us." While it was still dark, we got back in the car and headed back to Virginia.

10

The Rainbow

On that day, I needed my
heavenly father more than ever before.

It was a sad day, saying Good-bye to my beloved dad. I had walked in his steps all my life, and now he was gone. Dad would be missed by his many friends and neighbors and fellow-believers in the Colony. Dad had served the Colony for over forty years as pastor and bishop. Cousin George III spoke at the memorial service. He said, "The Colony will never be the same for me, now that Uncle Truman is gone."

The singing was beautiful that day. Dad's good friend, Myron Ross, led the congregation in singing the songs the family had selected: "How Firm a Foundation," "Children of the heavenly Father," "Precious Lord, Take My Hand," "I Am the Bread of Life (And I Will Raise You Up)," "In the Rifted Rock I'm Resting," "Gentle Shepherd, Come and Lead Us."

There was a time of remembrance, and we were blessed with the stories and tributes for my father. I read a poem I had found a few months before that reminded me of Dad. It was written by Georgia Harkness. Titled "To My Father," the first line of the poem I read back then was "A giant pine, magnificent and old. . . ." Now here, inspired by Harkness, is my version:

My dad was a giant of a man.
Now he was forever gone.
Most of his adult years he had lived among the giant pines of
    Tidewater, Virginia.
He built our home in the midst of a pine grove. Occasionally
we would experience monster storms—I remember one storm
where five giant pine trees were uprooted, torn from the ground.
Irreplaceable giants, and the landscape was forever changed.

Now Dad was gone, and the landscape was changed forever.
Dad's life would speak with a new urgency and integrity.
It was fitting now to read the poem and remember Dad as
"a giant pine, magnificent and old."

The whole congregation, as one body, followed the pall-bearers across the road, into the cemetery, to the plot prepared. We sang, "Shall We Gather at the River?"

The words of committal were spoken, another prayer was prayed. Just as we were leaving the graveside to return to the church, someone cried, "Look at the rainbow!"

God is amazing. That rainbow sign of hope came just when we needed it most. On that day I needed my heavenly Father more than ever before.

There were more stories. Oliver Hertzler, who lives near the church, told me, "The day your father died, there was a magnificent rainbow over Brother Truman's house."

God is amazing! A few days later, we had to say good-bye to Mom and drive back to Pennsylvania. Just a few miles out of the Colony, a magnificent rainbow appeared to the right of the car, then moved to the left of the car. Sometimes we were driving straight through the rainbow. A January rainbow is a miracle! We needed the miracle.

I live with the assurance that the wall between this world and the next is incredibly thin. Just as God is a close friend, present with me, so my dear dad and mom are very close. I miss my father, but he lives on in my heart.

Genesis 9:14, 15. When I bring clouds over the earth and the rainbow is seen in the clouds, I will remember my covenant that is between me and you.

11

A New Beginning

The girls' grandfather said, "I believe I should be baptized again."

M any of the tasks of pastoring are so satisfying. I especially loved to teach the instruction classes that led to baptism. The young people were so eager to learn, and I was eager to teach. Sometimes we had twenty young people in a class.

What a privilege it was to be part of such a signal event in a young person's life. I remember the baptism of Jody and Marilea. They were cousins, and on the day of their baptism at Highland Retreat, a great number of their family members were present. It was a happy day.

In the weeks after their baptism, I had an unexpected visitor at the church office: the girls' grandfather. He explained that he had been touched by the baptism of his granddaughters. He said, "You know, Truman, it has been so long since my own baptism, I sometimes believe I should be baptized again."

This would be a first for me—baptizing a man in his seventies. I responded to Roy, "Why don't we pray about this for a few days and if your conviction persists, then we will have a baptism right here in the church office."

I prayed and reflected on this request of Roy's. I came to believe that if the way has been long and hard, baptism again could be a launching pad for a new life in Christ. One day that week, Roy knocked on the door. "My wife has come with me, and I want to be baptized."

I knocked on the other office doors, found all the warm bodies in the church, and invited them to our service. We gathered, shared testimonies, then I baptized the oldest person I had ever baptized. We felt the Spirit descend, and I believe that all of us in the room experienced renewal in our own souls.

Thank you, Roy, for being sensitive to the spirit within. Baptism is refreshment for the journey. I believe God said that day, "Roy, you are my beloved child, and I am well pleased with you."

"O happy day! When Jesus washed my sins away!"

Matthew 3:16, 17. And when Jesus had been baptized, just as he came up from the water, suddenly the heavens were opened to him and he saw the Spirit of God descending like a dove and alighting on him. And a voice from heaven said, "This is my Son, the Beloved, with whom I am well pleased."

12

Child Dedication

"Please don't let him go to heaven yet!"

Sometimes the pastoral role is pure gift. Child dedications for me were a little bit of heaven. The young parents would stand before the congregation, holding their little treasure to be dedicated. The little tiny boy or girl,

So pure and good,
    So sweet-smelling and fresh-powdered,
        Straight from heaven and sinless.

Older siblings and Grandparents were invited to come forward and surround the little one being dedicated. Mommy and Daddy would introduce their baby to the congregation and try to put into words just how unique and precious was this particular child. Sometimes they would read a poem, quote a Scripture passage, or even sing a song for the little one.

At the appointed time, the parents would hand the baby for me to hold for the prayer of dedication. Then I would present the child to the congregation and add a few words to the baby: "See all these people? They are your spiritual aunts and uncles! See the children. They are your brothers and sisters! We are your family!"

With babies and children you can never guarantee your planned program. Once when the parents handed me their baby boy, his three-year-old sister cried out, "Please don't let him go to heaven yet!" Don't we wish we could see through the eyes of a child?

Child dedication is all about presenting a child to the Holy Community as well as to God. Perhaps it is not too far-fetched to believe an infant enters heaven at the time of dedication. The congregation would always respond "Yes," we receive this child as new life among us. We will, with the parents, bring the child up to love and serve God.

Reading from the back of the hymnal we would promise humbly to share in nurturing the child and to support, through prayer and our own examples and words, their efforts to provide a loving home centered on God's ways.

For all of us, participating in the dedication of a child was a special time to rededicate ourselves and our own children to be God's people.

13

Silent Cries
and Butterflies

*"God provided the symbol I needed
to recover my faith."*

Was that crying I heard outside the office door? I stepped over to open the door and found Jody, our administrative assistant. Jody was usually poised and gracious through the most trying situations. But here she stood sobbing, trying to compose herself to share the bad news.

Her nephew in Ohio had just been killed in a freak accident. Andy was a new Bluffton College graduate, and it was his first day at his summer job. Of course Jody was devastated. We prayed together for courage, hope, and faith in this hard time.

At graduation, Andy decided to take a year off from further studies to find his mission in life, while his girlfriend Angie finished college. He found work with a construction company. While Andy was helping to remove a tree, some equipment broke and hit him on the head, causing his immediate death.

Stunned with grief, Angie went alone to Andy's room. In his stereo was the tape he had been playing the night before. Angie pushed "play" and heard words from "The Cry" speaking of being free from fears and tears upon going to see the Lord.

Jody and her husband drove to Ohio to be with Andy's family and attended the memorial service. The church could not hold all who came. Classmates and family were there to support Andy's family and his girlfriend Angie.

At the graveside his Bluffton classmates circled the casket with its large spray of flowers. They linked arms and softly sang one of their college songs: "Kum-bah-yah, My Lord." When the service was over, no one moved. Then out of the immensity of space, down from the sky, fluttered a huge, Monarch butterfly. It lit for one moment on a flower then ascended into the blue. It was an epiphany. God was at the funeral!

When Jody returned home, she shared with us the story that follows, and read to us the poem Andy had written just a few days before his death. Read at his funeral, it was called "Butterflies and Silent Cries."

Butterflies and Silent Cries

Then I ask Jesus, "Why are those two always there?"
*   To which he replies, "They show how deeply you care."*
I thank him and praise him,
*   Bringing tears to my eyes: "Are you happy, my son?"*
It no longer matters . . . as long as I have those
*   Butterflies and silent cries.*
But we still need that peace that only Jesus can give,
*   To be joyous and kind, to love and to live,*
There'll always be things that bring tears to our eyes.
*   Are we happy? Yes, because of his love.*
And it's okay to have butterflies and silent cries."
—Andy Lehman

Jody's son, Caleb, was a special friend of Andy. Some months after Andy's death, Caleb tried to explain his response to the tragedy: "I felt we had been betrayed by the Creator of Life. On that day, my relationship with God was shaken. All I knew was that God was not there. I was angry and upset. No words or touch could comfort me."

Caleb described again the appearance of the butterfly, and he recalled that

> It was a moment I will never forget! It felt to me like God, in his deepest compassion, was looking down on us, and seeing us in such grief couldn't help himself, and had to send us a sign to tell us he loves us and is present with us.
>
> It was the symbol I needed to recover my faith.

Isaiah 43:1, 2. I have called you by name, you are mine. When you pass through the waters, I will be with you; and through the rivers, they shall not overwhelm you.

14

An Invitation to Build

"Dear Lord, please send us a wren."

Gertrude loved wrens and thought how gratifying it would be if she could have a little wren in her own backyard. She said to Eric, "I have always wanted a wren house. If you build a house, maybe a wren will come. I'd like it right here in front of the kitchen window."

Eric and Gertrude had lived together and had raised their family at this place. They had never seen a wren on their property, but Eric knew about Gertrude's revelations. If Gertrude needed a wren house, it was time to build, no questions asked.

The little bird house was built and installed right outside the kitchen window. Gertrude stood at her kitchen counter, preparing sandwiches and drinks for lunch. She prayed, "Dear Lord, please send us a wren!"

She opened her eyes. There was the wren, investigating the new house.

This was not the only lesson I learned from this petite Swiss woman. Gertrude spoke in a heavy accent, for she had come to America as an adult. She was a professional baker at the local grocery store.

One early morning she appeared at our front door bearing a loaf of bread, warm from her oven. We knew that her bread was perfection. I thanked her profusely for the gift, then added, "If I know you, you have probably prayed over this bread."

She replied, "Truman, I have never baked a loaf of bread without praying a blessing for those who will eat it."

It is said that the great artist Michelangelo, accompanied by his apprentice, went to have a drink one night with another artist. The whole evening the artists talked about where to get the best paint pigments, how to mix them, how to sharpen chisels, where to find the best marble.

When they were walking home, the apprentice said to Michelangelo, "I came along to learn about great art by listening to you talk about it. All you talked about was a hundred little details." Michelangelo replied, "Oh, we did talk about great art, my young friend. Great art is made of a hundred little details."

Isn't that how it is with the church? A great church is made up of hundreds of details. Small obediences. Constant in prayer. Outdoing one another in loving.

Some people sweeten our lives.

Some people sweeten our churches.

Gertrude is one such person.

15

Have Mercy
on Me, O Lord!

*I begged God hundreds, thousands
of times, over and over, day after day.*

The children poured into the church office after Sunday school. They knew there was a standing invitation to come in for a lollipop. This was one of my favorite "duties." It was a way to have personal contact with all the little ones young enough and brave enough to come through the door.

On this particular morning, I was not feeling up to par. It was a relief to get through the sermon and return to my office to prepare for the onslaught of children. I had gone to see my doctor three times during the week, complaining of sharp ear pains. Each time, he took another look at my ears, washed out my ears, and prescribed antibiotics and ear drops. Still the pain continued.

Dr. Jeff Wilkins, a member of the congregation, stood at the door of the church office, waiting for his son to come and claim a lollipop. Betty said to Jeff, "What is wrong with Truman—he hasn't been feeling well all week, and he looks funny!"

Jeff took one look and replied, "He has shingles." Jeff called the pharmacy so we could pick up the prescription on the way home. He warned me that this was expensive medicine, but that it might keep the shingles from getting worse. He explained that the main thing is to start treatment immediately. This was discouraging news—I realized I was at least ten days late getting started on medication. We stopped at the drugstore, picked up the $150 package, and I took the first dose.

But treatment had come too late. When shingles are not treated early, they can lead to complications in the nervous system. By Tuesday of that week, I was experiencing strange sensations in the right side of my face. My right eye would not close, and my mouth sagged. I was sent to a neurologist. He diagnosed Bells Palsy and warned, "You might have to fight this condition for up to five years."

It seemed like the end of the world. I asked for a leave of absence from preaching. In the days that followed, I prayed for a miracle. I was persistent as I knocked on the doors of heaven. I took the words of Psalm 51 as my mantra and prayed hundreds, even thousands of times, over and over, day after day: "Have mercy on me, O Lord."

Ten days later I woke up a healed man. The right side of my face had returned to normal. My eye could open and close, and I could smile on both sides of my face. Never again will I take good health for granted. How can I ever repay God's goodness! Thank you, Thank you, Thank you, Lord.

Psalm 51:1-15. Have mercy on me, O God, according to your steadfast love. O Lord, open my lips, and my mouth will declare your praise.

16

A Prayer for Charles

He had been a natural, playing the role of Jesus in Godspell.

The prayer for Charles started with an invitation: "Truman, our family is in pain. Tomorrow Charles leaves for college. We're not handling it very well. Could you come and help us say good-bye to him?"

It was truly a pastoral occasion, and I readily accepted the invitation. Charles would indeed by missed by his family. As the eldest son of his parents, and the elder brother of Kirsten and Mike, he would leave a huge vacancy in the family.

He was also a favorite at church—a good singer, an active member of the youth group, and friendly with old and young. He had played the role of Jesus in *Godspell* that summer and had been a natural. He would be sorely missed by all of us.

We stood in a close circle in the Peachey living room. First Urbane and Gwen, then sister and brother gave their tearful blessings to Charles. When it started getting too weepy, Charles disarmed us all when he responded, "After all, I'm just going to Goshen! I will be home for Christmas!" We laid hands on Charles and prayed for God's abundant mercy and care.

Charles was a good student and had four wonderful years at Goshen College. He married beautiful and talented Marcy and they moved to Philadelphia for graduate studies. The future looked bright.

Charles took care of his physical health—he regularly jogged through the city. One day when he was out running, he fell to the pavement. The diagnosis: a virus had attacked the lining of his heart, and survival would depend on receiving a heart transplant. Charles waited and waited for his new heart, but he died before a new heart became available.

I received word of his tragic death and was asked to return to Akron to help with the memorial service. We wept together; the pain was almost unbearable. But it was somehow comforting to remember the way Charles' family had granted him a blessing. Charles knew that he was loved unconditionally.

Even in their terrible grief, his family is reassured with memories of a blessed son.

Psalm 121:7- 8. The Lord will keep you from all evil; he will keep your life. The Lord will keep your going out and your coming in from this time on and forevermore.

17

A Final Act of Blessing

Mary breathed a prayer of unconditional love on her daughter.

Mary was at death's door. Her cancer had progressed beyond all hope. The church had prayed; Mary and Dan and their family and friends had been diligent and faithful in praying for her healing. Now the family gathered every evening in her hospital room, expecting this to be the day when she would take her last breath.

Mary and Dan had raised their family on a quiet street in Souderton, Pennsylvania. They had two grown children—a son who had given them beautiful grandchildren, and a daughter Susan who lived in the fast lane. Susan had never married, and her parents did not approve of her lifestyle.

Now at the point of death, the family would gather, expecting death to come and release Mary from her pain. But Mary could not seem to die.

One day when Mary seemed more alert than usual, I brought up the subject of her alienation from Susan. I asked, "Mary, have you ever given a blessing to Susan? I know you have blessed your son and he has been a blessing to you. But what about Susan? Has she received a blessing from you? Would you like to bless Susan?" Mary thought this over and in a voice almost too weak to be heard, responded, "I would like to bless Susan."

That evening, the whole family once again gathered around Mary's bed. Mary reached toward her daughter, took Susan in her arms, and breathed a prayer of blessing on her.

In the next few hours, Mary slipped away to her heavenly home. She had taken care of the most important work of a parent—granting a blessing of unconditional love and acceptance to a child. Now Mary was free to go home, where her heavenly Father waited with open arms to embrace her and extend heaven's blessing.

The Lord bless you and keep you;
The Lord make his face to shine upon you,
   And be gracious to you;
The Lord lift up his countenance upon you,
   And give you peace.
         —Numbers 6:24-26

18

The Portrait

*Thirty years later, Betty
accepts with grace my loving gesture.*

Tom Schenk, the artist, was famous in the Mennonite community. He had been raised in a Mennonite family and knew the history and culture of the church. So when a church agency decided to have special artwork produced, Tom's name emerged.

He was the age of my parents, in fact had been the best man at their wedding. And he was Betty's first cousin. When he came through the Valley, he would park his van in our driveway and spend the evening with us.

I was planning a surprise birthday party for Betty's fortieth birthday. She had been my partner and inspiration in so much of my church work, and I wanted to show my appreciation. I thought of the perfect gift for this occasion—I would have Cousin Tom paint her portrait. Tom was eager to do the work, and at his request I put together a packet of recent photos for him to use in the project.

It was easy to find the photos. Betty was a schoolteacher, and every year she brought home another free school picture. On picture-taking days, she would wear her brightest colors. In a photo I particularly liked, she was wearing a navy blue sleeveless dress with bright red and white trim. This seemed to be the photo that Tom chose for his painting.

A few weeks before The Day, Tom drove into town bearing the finished portrait. He opened his van and with great pride unwrapped the portrait. He told me that when he began painting her eyes, the portrait seemed to come alive and talk back to him.

At first glance, the finished product made her look a little older than her forty years. But I thought, *Oh well, she will grow into it.* I had often heard Tom say that he did not like to paint a very young person. Without lines and without character, they were like an "unbaked loaf of bread." I noticed he had painted a few lines and some character into Betty's face.

The party was scheduled for 9:00 p.m., when Betty would get home from her evening class at James Madison University. The children were allowed to stay up late, and I had invited a whole roomful of neighbors and friends.

At the appropriate time I broke out the main attraction, unveiling The Portrait. I'm not sure what I expected, but from here on events did not follow my plan. Betty looked at the portrait like it was an awful thing, laughing and crying at the same time.

Our friends all knew that Tom had just finished painting the three martyrs of the church—Conrad Grebel, Felix Manz, and George Blaurach. Betty decided on the spot that Tom was so enamored with the martyrs that he continued the theme in this birthday portrait. Her red, white, and blue sleeveless dress had been turned into the deep purple and maroon tones of the martyrs' long-sleeved robes. And she reasoned that, because Tom liked her, he painted her as if she were his own peer. Instead of forty, she appeared to be sixty.

As the evening wore on, she put aside her concerns about the unwanted portrait and the expense, and joined in the fun. We decided then and there that this portrait had had its unveiling; now it would be veiled.

Thirty years later, Betty believes the lines on her face have caught up with the lines in the portrait. At age seventy she has matured enough to accept with grace my loving gesture and the careful detailed work of Cousin Tom.

Every now and then we bring the portrait into the light of day. When we do this, I am reminded that the best intentions can go awry. Initially the portrait caused more pain than joy. Now, perhaps, it is achieving its intended purpose—to honor my beloved wife, and to thank her for being my lover and soul-mate.

19

An Anniversary to Remember

"Thoughtful and patient, tender and tough, surprising and playful."

Sunday would be our fortieth anniversary, and we decided to take a leave of absence from the pulpit. It could be covered by a visiting speaker.

This would give me a sense of solidarity with the lay members of the church. We had heard before coming to Pennsylvania that we could expect the attendance to be up and down. This was accompanied by chuckles, as people would explain that the congregation would often be "up in the mountains and down at the shore."

This was new to us—the folks in our home church in Virginia didn't seem to take that many vacations. But here in Pennsylvania we came to accept the up-and-down attendance. And this particular day, we were among those away.

During my seminary days, I had taken some of my coursework at Union Theological Seminary in New York City. During my weeks in the city, I would often attend Riverside Church, where Dr. James Forbes was the pastor. I learned to love and appreciate and respect this wonderful preacher.

So on this fortieth anniversary, Betty and I gave ourselves permission to drive into the city that Sunday morning to hear Dr. Forbes. He was in his usual good form, and we were in a relaxed mood to just sit and listen and be close to each other.

Midway through his sermon, he explained that this was his and Betty's thirtieth anniversary and he had written a special song for her! He began to sing, "What kind of love were you dreaming of?"

We remember some of the words that followed, "Thoughtful and patient, tender and tough, surprising and playful, but never too rough." He sang and we were moved and blessed. It seemed like it could have been our song.

After the benediction was pronounced, we joined the line of worshipers waiting to greet Dr. Forbes. We expressed our delight and explained that it was our anniversary, too, and that we were making his song our song.

Hearing this, Dr. Forbes reached up with both arms, made a little canopy over the two of us, and prayed a gentle blessing on our marriage. It was one of our most blessed anniversaries, and we still hold it close.

20

A Birthday Party Turned Upside Down

We cling to God, resting in his care, asking for help and healing.

In the year of our Lord 1996, I would turn sixty-five. I was not entirely pleased at the thought. I wanted to keep on working! I thought I had more wisdom and patience and long-suffering than ever before, but here I was reaching retirement age.

Betty sensed that we needed help to get through this birthday. She planned a special party, inviting friends near at hand and from the Lancaster area.

Her first call was to Rowland Shank, my cousin living near Hershey, Pennsylvania. When Rowland and Thelma accepted the invitation, Betty called Don and Martha Augsburger in Lancaster and suggested the two couples might ride together.

On Sunday afternoon, May 19, 1996, the celebration began. All the local guests arrived, and we relaxed with appetizers and munchies. We knew those traveling a longer distance might arrive late.

But when the phone rang, it was Don. He had just received a call from Lancaster General Hospital. Rowland and Thelma had been in an accident, a head-on crash, and been taken by ambulance to the hospital. Their injuries were serious. Don told us he was heading to the hospital to see the Shanks and promised to keep us informed. The party atmosphere turned into a time of concern and prayerfulness.

How quickly plans can change! Rowland and Thelma recovered, but Thelma had to undergo many surgeries and still suffers effects of the accident. We had expected to move back to the Valley for our retirement years, and Rowland and Thelma carried out their plans of doing likewise. Now we attend the same church, often eat lunch together, and sometimes play dominos at our dining room tables.

We take courses together through the Life-Long Learning Institute at James Madison University, most recently hiking the Appalachian Trail while our instructor explained the geological marvels of our region. If I need help pruning a fruit tree, I call on Thelma or Rowland for help. If my sheep find a weak place in the fence, I can count on Rowland's expert help.

Thelma and Rowland's house is lovely, beautifully decorated, and impeccable. Just today, Betty said to me, "Why don't you bring that garden hose in from the yard? You know Rowland would never leave something lying around like that." And of course, I could say, but I wouldn't think of saying, "How did this room get this messed up? You know it wouldn't look like this at Rowland and Thelma's house!" It's fun to have retired cousins nearby!

We are so vulnerable in our human situation. We remember my sixty-fifth birthday, the sun at our backs, sharing the day with good friends in a happy adventure. Then we hit a blue patch during which the sun is not shining. We cling to God in prayer, believing in his care and faithfulness. We ask for help and healing, not only for ourselves and our family, but for our many friends and beyond that for the community and our brothers and sisters all over the world.

Psalm 90:12. So teach us to number our days, that we may apply our hearts unto wisdom.

21

A Golden Jubilee

*The square dance was at the end of the
evening so some could leave early.*

June was rapidly approaching, and we were still saying we did
not want a celebration. We had been to dozens of golden
wedding anniversaries, had sat at beautifully decorated tables,
looked at old photos of the bridal couple, eaten peanuts and
white cake. Somehow these occasions seemed more like funerals.

And they were always on Sunday afternoon when most
guests would rather be at home snoozing in front of the game.
So we kept telling our children that we definitely did not want
a fifty-year anniversary celebration.

During the Christmas season we were invited to a square
dance and had a wonderful time. The idea came to us, Why
don't we plan a barn happening?

We knew that Harley Showalter rented his barn for community events. We would invite Ralph Hill's bluegrass group,
we would have Smokin' Pig cater the barbecue supper. We
would ask Jana and Jerry Zirkle to call a square dance and teach
all of us a few basic steps. We along with our children and
grandchildren would wear overalls and denim for a family
photo.

The planning became fun instead of duty. Lowell Byler designed and printed on his computer the invitations that depicted a barn and silo. Don would be the emcee, Kathy would play the keyboard. Her family put together a special songbook for the sing-along.

We asked Beryl to speak words of blessing and wanted to repeat our vows. We also wanted to include something about our fiftieth anniversary as an echo of the biblical year of Jubilee, when old hurts are forgiven and all things made new.

Our small group offered to help with the details. Liz insisted that we find Betty's wedding dress and wedding photo so that she could arrange a table of mementos. The women helped set up tables and the men stood at the road to direct parking.

Betty's brother Maurice came a day early from Colorado and helped to arrange pots of red geraniums. It was such an honor that *all* our brothers and sisters came, including Dave's all the way from Idaho. Close friends arrived from their homes in Pennsylvania and Indiana.

As the guests arrived, the bluegrass group sang and played. We ate supper at long tables. Then we gathered for the serious part of the evening—ten minutes of blessing and remembering and repeating our vows. Don kept things moving with his natural wit and sense of timing. Then we handed out the songbooks. It was our party. We could have singing. Kathy kept the music at a fast tempo and the bluegrass group played along. We sang all the way through a dozen of "our" songs: "Let Me Call You Sweetheart," "Remember Me," "Amazing Grace," "Keep on the Sunny Side," "Down to the River to Pray," "Goodnight Irene." That last one had to have an explanation.

After we sang it was time for the square dance. We knew that some of our guests would be uncomfortable with this part, so we had planned this to be at the end of the evening. Those who needed to could leave at that time.

We never had so much fun at a golden anniversary celebration! It was a reminder to us that we have been lucky in love, and we are dedicated to making our golden years a time of looking forward, not backward. We make every effort to spend more time with young people than with old people. We thank the Lord for this precious time of life together.

22

O Happy Day!

*Now I can say I have been
baptized by pouring and by immersion*

Betty and I were finally on our way to the West Coast. All cares and duties were left behind. It was time to celebrate, see our beautiful country, enjoy time alone.

We had wonderful, uninterrupted conversations and sometimes rode in silence. We had mapped out our itinerary, but loosely, so we could change whatever needed changing anytime.

We had already heard the country singers and seen *The Shepherd of the Hills* at Branson, Missouri. We were headed for the train in Williams, Arizona, that would take us to Grand Canyon. After that it would be California and the redwood forests, the Oregon coast where we would pick Marion berries, Seattle where we would attend a wedding, British Columbia, and then Idaho and Colorado for visits with brothers.

Somewhere in California, our cell phone rang; it was son-in-law Dean. After filling us in on family news, he came to the point. Would we be willing to meet them at Lake Michigan for a baptism service? Dean and son, Andrew, age fourteen, would both like to be baptized.

I was elated! I had often wondered where Dean stood in his spiritual pilgrimage. This was an answer to prayer. I suggested that Dean invite some friends from the Methodist church in Ohio where he, Kathy, and family attend.

Three weeks later, we stood along the shores of Lake Michigan with Dean and Kathy, Andrew and Adrienne. Also present were elders and the praise group from Hope Methodist Church who had come to support Dean and Andrew in this step of faith.

We had decided to meet early in the morning, before the shore activities got underway. We sang and prayed together. About this time, I noticed the ocean-like waves on this lake. I had never thought of a lake having whitecaps, but this was a lively lake.

Dean and Andrew had let me know they wanted to be immersed. Backward! I believe that all forms of baptism are good, but looking at that choppy lake made me wonder how I was going to handle these big men in this choppy surf.

I stepped over and asked a big, husky Methodist named Tom to accompany us in the water, just in case we needed extra support.

The four of us walked into the lake. Dean would be baptized first. I had just said the words, "I baptize you in the name of the Father, and the Son, and the Holy Spirit." A huge wave hit. We were all four swept under. We pulled ourselves together and proceeded with the baptism of Andrew. Seagulls were circling, the lighthouse nearby was signaling its light, and Hope Methodist Church Praise Band was singing on shore when we baptized Dean and Andrew and gave them to the Lord.

"O Happy Day! O Happy Day! When Jesus washed my sins away!" Now I can say I have been baptized by pouring and by immersion! It was a high moment of my life.

23

I'll Fly Away, O Glory

The cowboy and I were singing a duet!

The steam engine huffed and puffed its way across the Arizona mountains. We were on our way to the Grand Canyon and were being treated to live entertainment by cowboys with guitars.

Good friends Michael and Peggy had told us about their vacation experience on this special railway located in Williams, Arizona, nestled in the mountains of northern Arizona.

The brochure said, "Make your Grand Canyon vacation unforgettable. Step back in time to the days when cowboys roamed the dusty plains of the Wild West and train travel was the prominent means of transportation to the Grand Canyon. Hop aboard a vintage 1923 Pullman coach for a 65-mile awe-inspiring train journey. . . . "

We had followed our friends' instructions and were now seated on this old train, without a care in the world. The ride to the Canyon would last about an hour, and here was this singing cowboy. Other passengers were requesting special songs, and we would all join in with the singing.

When the cowboy stood next to our seat, I asked, "Do you know 'I'll Fly Away'?" He stood right at my shoulder, and when he heard me singing the melody, he switched to tenor harmony.

I always said I couldn't sing, because I would end up singing melody when all the other men sang bass. I just hadn't got the knack of harmonizing. But here we were—the cowboy and I singing a duet! We sang all the song, written by Kanye West: "Some glad morning when this life is o'er, I'll fly away. . . ."

This was my moment in the sun! At the end of the song, the cowboy got right in my face, and said, ""Wow! You have a beautiful baritone voice." O Happy Day! I've been singing ever since, sometimes melody and sometimes harmony, but I will always remember that in the seventy-first year of my life, I sang beautifully.

24

Three More Dimes, Quick!

Within minutes, I returned to the vows I'd made to be a patient husband.

We were on our way to the West Coast culminating in the wedding in Seattle of our friend's son. We were traveling in my new Toyota Tundra pickup. High off the ground, just as comfortable as our car, it seemed a better choice for seeing the countryside. The first few days I said to myself, "I'm going to be in this little space capsule for the next thirty days. Lord, make me kind, loving, patient, every hour, every day."

We had done all the touristy things; now Seattle and the wedding on Whidbey Island would be our next event. The wedding invitation had noted that the wedding meal would be catered but that guests could bring something for the dessert buffet. As we neared the site of the wedding, we talked about what kind of dessert we could purchase.

We had been seeing the wild berries growing along the coastal highways. When we stopped for lunch, the parking lot of the diner was rimmed with these same wild berries. The natives called them Marion berries, but it seemed the natives were ignoring them.

After lunch we walked along the edge of the lot and filled two small buckets with the luscious berries. These would be our dessert offering! We proudly carried them to the wedding and handed them over to the caterers. We saw one of the servers reach up and put the berries on a shelf, as if they could be a decoration. But when I came through the line, I reached up and placed the buckets on the table. Soon they were eaten up by the guests—we had made our contribution to the dessert buffet.

To this point, the Lord had answered my prayer. I had indeed been the model husband. We were now on the last leg of our trip. We approached Chicago from the south side. Betty was driving the Toyota; the highways were broad, with multiple lanes and lots of traffic. We were fast approaching a toll booth. Long lines of vehicles were at a standstill, waiting their turn. One car at a time, we inched toward the booth, and at the last minute noticed the "Exact Change" sign.

"Quick, find thirty cents!" I heard Betty say, and I scrambled. I handed her three dimes, she rolled down the window, pitched the coins. Not one hit the basket. The red light came on; the barricade stayed put. Horns blew. "Quick, quick, more dimes!"

By some miracle I found more dimes. This time she leaned out the window and carefully dropped the coins into the basket. We pulled away from the scene, and I said a bad word. Three bad words.

Betty said nothing. Within fifteen minutes I had recovered, returning to the vows I had made about being a thoughtful and patient husband.

Maybe life would get boring without these tense, frantic, moments. In reliving our wonderful trip to the West Coast, this is one of my favorite stories. From this distance, it seems hilarious.

25

A House Built on Trust (Sermon)

*I remember the first time
divorce happened in my circle of friends.*

I stopped by the house to welcome the young couple back to their hometown and to invite them to church. They had been gone for several years and had just returned. By now they had two young children, Laura and Michael, who looked forward to living near both sets of grandparents.

I had called ahead and expected to be greeted by husband and wife. Instead, Rachel stood in the doorway with her two children. All three were crying while Rachel tried to explain. Just the day before, her husband had packed his things and stood in this doorway saying good-bye. He was leaving his family. As he left, he picked up his three-year-old daughter and said, "Laura, you take good care of Mommy."

Laura broke into tears and cried, "I'm too little to take care of Mommy."

For Laura and Michael, ages three and two, in a sense their childhood was over. Life would never be the same. A household with two parents having meals together, sharing fun times and vacations, learning to work and play together—all over.

Yes, there were grandparents and aunts and uncles. And a mommy who did her best to hold things together. But their hearts were broken the day Daddy left.

The tragedy of divorce is difficult to talk about. Many in the church have been through the agony of having a mate leave the marriage. Some have lived in abusive situations in which they themselves finally made the decision to leave.

Some of us have lived through the divorce of our children. I've had friends in their golden years say this is the most difficult experience of their whole life—standing by while a child suffers through divorce.

If you were raised the way I was, you were taught that marriage is forever, and that divorce is almost the unforgivable sin. And that, no matter what, a Christian must never consider the possibility of remarriage. In Malachi 2:16 we read, "For I hate divorce, says the Lord the God of Israel. . . ."

This was the Old Testament Jesus taught from. But then Jesus teaches, in the Beatitudes of the New Testament, that there is forgiveness of sins. Blessed are the poor in spirit, blessed are the brokenhearted. Who fits the Beatitudes more perfectly than the person who has experienced a failed marriage? Blessed are the divorced and remarried who acknowledge their sins, repent of them, and believe the gospel of full forgiveness of sin.

When I have been asked to participate in a second marriage, I have needed to hear the story of what went wrong. Sometimes the previously married person tries to explain the divorce, or excuse the divorce, or in some way minimize the failure of the earlier marriage. Of these persons I ask, "Was there sin? Is there repentance?" Real sins and repentant sinners can be forgiven. If there was no sin, and no repentance, then there can be no forgiveness.

I remember the first time divorce happened in my circle of friends. Rex and Sue were in their thirties; we had been acquainted since high school days and had shared meals in each other's homes. I thought we knew each other well.

I was in seminary in Richmond when I heard about Rex leaving his family. This seemed impossible! How could a decent moral man like Rex just walk out on his family! I called Rex, and he agreed to meet with me. I rode the bus to Newport News, and we spent an hour together. I pleaded with him to change his mind, but it was no use. He was saying good-bye to his wife and daughter. No way was he turning back!

Do you remember when you thought that a good marriage
could be built on romantic love?
Romantic love is . . . romantic!
It happens easily and naturally.
We "fall in love."
We believe that this person is perfect.
We are blind to any faults or imperfections.

In *Ragman and Other Cries of Grace*, Walter Wangerin writes, "Love may begin a marriage; but love does not make a marriage. You will ride a wild sea, if you think you can build your marriage upon your love."

Instead of building on romantic love,
build on the covenant, the vows you make.
The covenant of marriage is the house that
holds our unpredictable hearts.
Marriage is the arena in which love comes,
love goes,
and love comes again.
(And while you wait for love to come again, you remember your
promise to each other.)

Thornton Wilder's play, *The Skin of Our Teeth,* is the drama of the Antrobus family. At a crucial moment in the play, Mrs. Antrobus confronts her husband with his betrayal and unfaithfulness. Her words describe the very foundations of marriage, as she explains that she didn't marry him because he was perfect but because he made her a promise. The Christian marriage ceremony acknowledges that—

We commit to God
  We commit to our partner
    We commit to the congregation.

Listen to the marriage vows we speak to each other:
Will you have this man (woman)
  to be your wedded husband (wife)?
    To live together in the holy estate of matrimony?
Will you love, comfort, honor keep. . . .
  In sickness and in health,
  and forsaking all others
  keep yourself only unto him (her)
  as long as you both shall live?

Then the bride and groom repeat their vows to each other:
"I take you to be my wedded wife (husband),
  To have and to hold,
    from this day forward—
for better, for worse,
  for richer or poorer,
    in sickness and in health,
      to love and to cherish,
        till death us do part,
          according to God's holy ordinance,
            and thereto I pledge you my faith."

These are the covenants we make. They are linked with the
covenants God has made with us. If we build on these, we are
building on a Rock! If we base our marriage on these promises,
our marriage will live!
Let's keep our covenants in front of us,
and renew them daily.
Listen to the way God keeps his covenants. Here is what he says:
  I will be your God!
    You will be my people!
      I will care for you and keep you.
        I will always be with you—walking by your side.
        I will be merciful and forgiving.

I will never forsake you,
I will love you tenderly,
With steadfast love.

Earlier, we referred to romantic love,
Based on feelings,
Blind to imperfections.
But we all know that one day we wake up!
We notice the imperfections,
the personal habits,
the little things that irritate.
And if marriage is built on romantic love,
we can just walk away,
and say, "We aren't compatible!"
Aren't we living in that kind of world?
Where we can just walk away?

Eric Fromm, noted Jewish psychologist, writes this description of how we set ourselves up for failure: "When you pick up one end of a stick, you pick up the other end as well."

A married man starts to notice a young woman in the office. He sees her as "Perfection, personality plus, so easy to be with. She understands me."

He writes down her phone number and tucks it away in his bill
fold.
It stays there for some weeks.
One day, when he's had an argument with his wife,
he remembers:
perfection,
personality plus,
easy to get along with.
He picks up the phone.
They meet for dinner and drinks,
a night together.
Where did it all begin?
When he tucked her telephone number into his billfold!
It was there that the whole "affair" was set into motion.

I read about a six-year-old girl in her new foster home. There had been a long line of foster homes. The new foster mother was tucking the little girl into bed for the first time,

The little girl asked her to take off her wedding ring so she could see it. The foster mother was reluctant but wanted to respond, then was startled when the little girl clutched the ring tightly, and put her little fist firmly under the pillow, and said, "There, now, you won't leave me while I'm sleeping."

When we make a promise, our behavior follows it.

Our actions strengthen and deepen the relationship.
> *Through acts of kindness,*
> *Through my words,*
> *Through a written note,*
> *Flowers in January,*
> *Time spent together.*
True happiness comes from giving myself away.
As Christians, we KEEP our promises:
> *We CAN be trusted.*
> *We are tenacious about COVENANTS.*
> *We are FAITHFUL.*
We can be DEPENDED upon.

Matthew 7:24,25. Everyone who hears these words of mine and acts on them will be like a wise man who built his house on rock. The rain fell, the floods came, and the winds blew and beat on that house, but it did not fall, because it had been founded on rock.

Part 3

BELOVED BROTHER JAMES

Stories of
Vocation and Grace

Part 3

Introduction

There is an important difference between preparing for a career and embracing a vocation. For me this has meant listening for a divine call and making a commitment to the prophetic teachings of the Bible concerning peace and justice. It has meant daring to dream and to take risks for the sake of Jesus. It has meant asking questions. It has meant saying "Yes" to Christ and then following with my life. I have heard a voice calling my name.

I believe this definition of vocation applies to all Christians. We are all called to our work. The ground on which we stand is Holy Ground. These words of Frederick Buechner have blessed me: "God calls you to the place where your deep gladness and the world's deep hunger meet." If we listen, God calls, and we move one step at a time in following him.

In the early years of our marriage, I received calls from various churches to come and be their pastor. This was in the time when men were called, not women. Churches were not necessarily looking for seminary-trained pastors but for men who seemed dedicated and willing to work for the church.

Each time another invitation would come, we gave it careful thought and prayer, and each time would decide that we were simply not prepared for such a major life change.

Twice we made the decision to attend our church college in the Shenandoah Valley, about four hours from our home in

Newport News, Virginia. But classes were difficult, money was scarce, and we were homesick. Both times, at the end of the semester, we packed up and went back home.

Ten years later, after completing I-W service in New Jersey, after six years of building homes in Newport News, and after adding two children, Kathy and Don to our family, the call came loud and clear. Together with Betty and children, I took on the challenge of relocating to the Valley and enrolling as a full-time college student.

This time, when Somebody called my name, I was ready to respond with a Yes. Never have I doubted the call or despaired of the calling.

The years since beloved Brother James tapped me on the shoulder in my youth have been filled with rich experiences. I thank God for the wonderful opportunities I have had to serve him. I would do it all again.

1

Somebody's Calling My Name (Sermon)

"I could easily see you in the ministry someday."

It was early Sunday morning, the sun just starting to appear, a few songbirds breaking into melody, a hint of frost on the lawn. I shivered as I waited. Then I heard it coming around the curve. The huge homely car ground to a stop. A back door swung open. I jumped in and the car lurched forward.

This car was just about the ugliest one ever made. The 1933 Terraplane seemed more tank than automobile. Its vast hood thrust forward into the dark road ahead. Already sitting on the spacious back seat was my best friend, Michael. Up front in the driver's seat was Brother James Bauman, our beloved Sunday school teacher. James had moved to our community from Canada when he married Alta Yoder.

The three of us, adult driver and two young passengers, were faithful members of Warwick River Mennonite Church. Michael and I, both twelve years old, were honest and pure. When an appeal was made for volunteers to distribute *The Way*, of course we signed up. *The Way* told how to be saved and live to the glory of God.

We were heading to downtown Newport News, about twelve miles away. We rode in silence for awhile, then out of the blue, Brother James tilted the rear-view mirror to look at both of us, cleared his throat and said, "Michael and Truman, I could easily see you in the ministry some day." We looked at each other and said nothing. I swallowed hard.

Finally we arrived in the residential area that was our destination. The sky was still dark. We did our work quickly. We wanted to be finished before the people woke up! Up and down flights of stairs in huge apartment buildings we flew. When we finally finished, the community was white with *The Way* pamphlet, as if a frost had settled. We climbed back into the big old tank and headed home.

In the years to come, Michael and I were tapped many times for the ministry, but the one who started the tapping was Brother James in his Terraplane. Both now in our seventies, Michael and I have served many years in the ministry. We say "thank you" to Brother James for calling us when we were only twelve years old.

William Barclay says there are two important days in your life: "The day you were born and / The day you understood why." I have known both. Someone called my name and my life has never been the same. Just as sure as I have heard my own call, I know each of you has been called: John, Susan, Mark, Carolyn. Whatever successes we have in life, I believe, will be measured by our answering that call.

Ultimately, Christ is our employer.

Christ is the one who sustains us. Who prays for us.

Christ is the one most hurt by our failures.

Recall that great moment in the Old Testament
when Moses, a stranger in exile,
*   murders an Egyptian.*

Death weighs on his conscience.
Impetuously, he has risked his fortune, his freedom, his future
    to save one solitary Hebrew slave.
For forty years shepherding sheep in a vast desert,
    already thinking about retirement.
Out of nowhere it explodes.
    A bush bursts into flames, crackling, leaping—
    and the bush is not consumed!

In that moment, he hears his name, "Moses, Moses."

Moses responds, "Here I am."
Demanding, life-changing words came next. "I AM! Go!"
There on a sand dune, sheep grazing all around,
    A man knelt in the desert
    and prayed and wrestled and cried.
    Until an old self died. Crucified.
    And a new self resurrected.
    Holy fire settled on him like Pentecost, filling, energizing,
        searing,
    Moses rose to his feet a new man!
    Ordained by God himself.
    The greatest leader of all time.
    One solitary man to stand against an empire.
    Empowered by God, Moses walked into Pharaoh's court,

With the flaming bush inside him.

From the quiet setting in the desert, Moses plunged into the
    whirlpool of history with the cry, "Let my people go!"
As Moses spoke, God worked, and the empire shook.

Only a short time later, the people complained, ungrateful,
    unwilling to be led.
    They had seen God work.
They had been freed from Egyptian bondage with miraculous signs
    and wonders.
        yet they had learned nothing.
Now, they are about to receive the call.

Not a burning bush, but a burning mountain!
And out of the mystery,
a voice calls. It is God, about to speak!

All of us are "on call." God places enormous loads on small shoulders. We drag our feet. We go with fear, We cry, "I cannot!"

But God whispers, "I am with you. I've chosen you. Be not afraid." Like the words in an old hymn:

How Firm A Foundation

Fear not, I am with thee, O be not dismayed,
For I am thy God and will still give thee aid.
I'll strengthen thee, help thee, and cause thee to stand,
Upheld by my righteous, omnipotent hand.

When through the deep waters I call thee to go,
The rivers of sorrow shall not overflow,
For I will be with thee, thy troubles to bless,
And sanctify to thee, thy deepest distress.

The soul that on Jesus hath leaned for repose,
I will not, I will not desert to his foes,
That soul, though all hell should endeavor to shake,
I'll never, no never, no never forsake.
—John Rippon

2

Musty Green Curtains

*The children's classes blended into
one holy crescendo.*

I remember the green curtains and musty smells of my earliest
Sunday school. The children's classes met in the basement.
After sitting with parents for the opening song, we children
were dismissed to go traipsing down the stairs. We could have
followed our noses, the basement smells were so musty.

There in our little cubicles, saintly teachers taught us about
God and his kingdom. I remember James Bauman, Alta Yoder,
Nelson Burkholder, and Nora Hostetter.

There were others, but these come to mind from the earliest years of my memory. They were so wise and old and holy
and perfect—it seemed to me they had just stepped out of the
Old Testament.

I was in a stage of faith development that allowed me to accept anything and everything spoken by my teacher as
TRUTH. How well I remember the Bible stories: Daniel and
the lions' den; the call of Samuel; the story of the Great Flood;
Jonah and the whale.

We were eager learners! These Bible stories formed the
foundation on which my faith would be built. Later I would
doubt and struggle but not now. These teachings were solid and

strong. What a basic foundation for future learning.

The basement could become a noisy place with all the classes blending into one holy crescendo. If things ever got boring, we could watch the feet of the children on the other side of the curtain, and hear what their teacher was saying.

When the bell rang, we climbed back upstairs to gather and sing in front of the congregation. Michael always requested "Dare to be a Daniel." Sometimes we sang "Be Careful, Little Hands, What You Do, Be Careful Little Feet, Where You Go." (I would be embarrassed, because my hands and feet and legs were never little.)

The holy mothers and fathers and aunts and uncles would beam their approval. We were blessed by the smiles of our elders, and we thought God was smiling, too.

3

A Little Sunshine

He walked west and came to a
beautiful green valley.

When Brother Jennings held revival meetings in our church, we welcomed him with open arms. While some visiting evangelists scared us into a response, Brother Jennings sweet-talked us into the kingdom. In such a gentle spirit he taught us about God's amazing grace.

At the beginning of each service, Brother Jennings would invite the children to come to the front for a story and singing. I remember a favorite song he taught us: "Jest a little sunshine, Jest a little chair, / Helps to make the rainbow now appear." We pictured a little rocking chair in a sunny corner. We came to realize we had misinterpreted Brother Jennings' accent! This southern gentleman wanted to teach us cheerfulness.

The older folks seemed to enjoy the children's stories, too. I'm sure there were several layers of lessons to be learned, and we children got part of the message. At the end of the week-long (or two-week-long) series, we all felt closer to God and at peace with our brothers and sisters. Brother Jennings' sweet and tender spirit drew us heavenward.

Years and years later, we became close friends with Brother Jennings' grandson, Chet Raber. Through Chet we heard the sad story of his grandfather's early life. William Jennings was born in Knoxville, Tennessee, the son of a military officer widower and his housekeeper.

William's presence in the home was a humiliation for the lady of the house, Emaline, his father's new wife. William was a reminder of her husband's unfaithfulness. Because of her rejection, William was never cared for by a true mother.

William's place at the table was far from the rest of the family. He ate in the kitchen and was expected to do the "mean" kitchen tasks. Instead of sleeping in a bed, he slept on a pile of rugs in the kitchen next to the stove. There he could keep the fire burning. Some say he was treated like a slave.

Despite Will's efforts to please, Emaline would scold and berate him with hostile comments. He lived with constant conflict and humiliation.

Finally, at age eighteen, the rejected, lonely young man gathered his possessions together and walked away from home. He walked west and came to a beautiful green valley near Concord. He did not know it was called "Dutch Valley" in recognition of the Pennsylvania Dutch Mennonites who came there to settle.

Will followed a long lane to a farmhouse and offered to work for food and shelter. The door was answered by Henry Good, a Mennonite farmer with long beard, wearing "plain" clothing. He offered work and told Will he could stay with the family.

Finally the homeless young man had a home! William ate at the family table. His situation improved even more when he realized that Anna, the Good's daughter, noticed him and accepted his attentions. The two cared deeply for each other, and within a year made plans for marriage.

Together William and Anna served many years sharing the good news of the kingdom.

4

CirCUSSES and CarnEVILS

*The revivalist knew firsthand
about drinking, dancing, and carousing.*

When Brother James Bucher came to the Colony to hold
revival meetings, the church was full. We knew the services would be lively and that sinners would be saved.

Brother Bucher spoke without notes. This allowed him to
roam the church, up and down the aisles, peering down the
long pews in search of the person who might be under conviction. With his mane of white hair, bushy eyebrows, and eyes of
fire, he looked like Moses coming down from the mountain.
He got our attention.

Hardened sinners were invited by neighbors to come to the
revival meetings. Brother Bucher could spot these folks and
preach directly to them of fire and brimstone. But he could also
reach the children. It seemed he was looking directly at me. In
recent years I learned the dates of his visits to the Colony. He
came in 1938 and 1940, when I was seven and then nine years
old.

I was old enough to know I did not want to go to hell. I
wanted to be forgiven of my sins and made ready for heaven.

Along with the hardened sinners, we children would make our way down the aisle to make our peace with God.

Brother Bucher shared glimpses of his early life. No wonder he was so graphic when he described the life of the sinner! He had learned firsthand about the evils of worldly pleasures—drinking, dancing, carousing, going to carnEVILS and cirCUSSes.

In the book *Under God's Arrest,* Ida Boyer Bontrager writes about Brother Bucher's conversion. At the time of their baptism, he and wife, Fannie, told each other and the Lord they wanted to be "stepping stones" and not "stumbling blocks" in the church.

James Bucher became serious about living the Christian life and encouraging others to come into faith. He was a persuasive, no-nonsense preacher. When Brother Bucher became an evangelist, he traveled across the country in a home-made housetrailer. Gospel messages painted on the trailer admonished, PREPARE TO MEET THY GOD, and REPENT AND BELIEVE THE GOSPEL.

One time when Brother Bucher held meetings in Elida, Ohio, he began his sermon with a little joke and elicited a chuckle from the congregation. After the service, Bishop J. M. Shenk reprimanded him, saying, "You know there was limited response tonight. I believe your joke was the reason." Brother Bucher held his head in shame.

Sometimes when I remember the revival meetings and fire and brimstone preaching from my childhood, I have said, "We are they who came through the Great Tribulation." Childhood faith. Old-time religion! I am thankful for the old-time evangelists who were part of my stepping-stones into a growing faith.

5

Plain and Tall

My new, custom-tailored suit did not fit!

In our community, wearing a "plain suit" meant that you had accepted the doctrine of nonconformity. Ordering a plain suit was also a rite of passage. It was part of leaving childhood and becoming a responsible member of the community.

I was becoming a man and was eager to take my place among the men of the Colony. So that morning when my father cleared his throat and said, "Son, I believe it is time to order a plain suit for you," I perked up my ears. I wanted to please my parents and the church. The thought of a new suit sounded good, too. I replied, "Yes, I am ready."

A few weeks later, Dad and I drove to the church where Jacob Martin had set up shop and was measuring men and boys for their new plain suits. He came from Martin's Store in the Shenandoah Valley, a store that specialized in plain clothing for the Mennonites in the Valley.

We flipped through the little patches of fabric and found a light blue material and chose it for my new suit. At thirteen, my first tailor-made suit!

Then peach season arrived, and all we could think about was the peaches and how to get them picked and off to market before they spoiled. I quickly forgot about new suits.

But when summer was over, and life had returned to nor-mal, the call came that our suits had arrived. We could come to the church to pick them up. With great anticipation Dad and I drove to the church. When it was my turn, Mr. Martin handed me my new suit, and I went to the side room to try it on.

It looked a little smaller than I expected. When I stepped into the pants, what a jolt I got! The pant-legs were six inches too short, the sleeves reached half-way between elbow and wrist. My new tailored-to-fit suit did not fit! Mr. Martin of-fered to take it back to the Valley and let out the seams and lengthen the pants. He did the best he could, but it was always a miserable fit.

I do remember that the fabric was very good—*serviceable* was the word. Sometimes I joke about it and say that my first suit was made of "steel-belted" material like good tires, and that even now, sixty years later, it probably lives on.

I wore that new blue suit and I became a man among other men that I admired. Sometimes I wish I had saved that original suit—it is the only custom-tailored suit I have ever owned!

6

Mom Didn't Believe in Women Pastors

*She prepared sermon outlines
for Dad and left them on his desk.*

Mom did not believe in women pastors. She expressed her beliefs firmly when she and I would discuss this question.

Dad did not feel the same way. He believed, as I do, that if a woman is called to preach, then she needs to preach! Dad was an early advocate of women in ministry.

Mom did believe in teaching. For forty-five years she taught Sunday school classes. She loved to study Scripture. She seemed to follow in her father's footsteps when it came to reading and studying.

When Dad and Mom were in their late forties, the family moved for a year to Harrisonburg, Virginia, so that my younger sister and I could attend Eastern Mennonite High School and so they themselves could take some Bible courses.

I learned later that my older sis, Evelyn, had planned to attend college that year but gave it up when she learned of our parents' intentions. She thought it was way too humiliating to be caught in the same college as her parents.

Dad and Mom enrolled in college and seminary classes—taking heavy courses like Old Testament History, Greek, and Hebrew. Mom would make straight A's while Dad would settle for A's and B's. Studying was not his great strength.

For most of his life, Dad served in various roles of Virginia Mennonite Conference. For seventeen years he was moderator of the conference and for several years moderator of the nation-wide Mennonite Church. This meant lots and lots of trips away from home. He was good at building relationships between people with differing points of view. And his gifts were widely used.

Dad was also a pastor at home in the Colony, which meant that he would need to have a sermon ready by Sunday morning. I remember the many times he would come home to find his sermon outline on the desk, complete with Scripture references, illustrations, poems, and hymns. Not many people in the Warwick River Church knew that the sermon they heard Dad preach on Sunday morning had been pulled together by Mom.

I never heard my parents discuss with each other the controversial issue of women in ministry. They both knew where the other stood on this question. The family knew that they held different opinions on various church issues.

I am sure my parents were supportive of each other in this area as with other issues in the church. There was no competition between them. They respected and encouraged each other and appreciated the many gifts each brought to the marriage.

I will add that one time I did hear about a major difference between the two. I was trying to talk Dad into not voting for President Nixon and heard Mom say, "It doesn't matter; when we go to the polls I plan to vote for the other side."

7

Called to Leave Home

*Betty and I still cry when we
remember that night.*

The voice would not go away. Betty and I had many conversations about a sense of call. How would the call come? How would we know for sure that it was from God? Would I be willing to return to school? I did not love studying. I loved hard physical labor, and I especially loved building houses.

By now we had two children, Kathy, age three, and Don, fifteen months. We knew that if we tried again to go to school, it would not be simple. It would be a huge undertaking—-we would have our beautiful house to sell, a hardworking carpenter crew to let go, and many, many friends and family members to say good-bye to.

Leaving the community this time was almost more than we could face. We couldn't imagine even telling our folks.

We made plans to spend a weekend in Harrisonburg. We would attend the spring oratorio, *The Holy City,* always a highlight of the year. We reserved rooms at a motel near Eastern Mennonite Collage. On the spur of the moment, I said to Betty, "Why don't we call George [the realtor who handled our houses] and ask him to list our house? If it sells, we'll know it's a sign that we can leave."

We gave George strict instructions not to advertise in the newspaper nor to let our families know about the listing. We also gave him the phone number of our motel, just in case he needed to contact us.

When we left for the Valley, the house was shining; a huge spray of dogwood stood inside the front door, and we thought it had never looked so beautiful. We loved this house.

We enjoyed the beautiful rendition of *The Holy City* and returned to the motel to get the children settled. The phone rang. It was George. He had been trying to reach us all evening.

A doctor from Germany was in town, looking for a house so he could send for his wife and family. He had cash and he wanted to buy. Did we really mean to be doing this? Yes, we had made up our minds.

We still cry when we remember that night. We had been dead serious when we called the realtor. We had needed some sign, some strong direction from God, and we believed this was a way to know for sure that we were to leave home and return to school.

But it hurt when we thought of leaving all our family and friends. We would have to live in the Valley for at least four years, and maybe we'd never return to our beloved Colony.

Our beautiful house was sold! We tried to keep as calm as possible so that the children would not sense our distress, but we were both shedding tears. How could we possibly get to sleep tonight? Betty suggested we take a ride, maybe find some place open late where we could get ice cream.

That September I was back in the classroom. It still was not easy for me to study; it seemed to take months before I could fit into the role of student. How often have I needed to remember that particular weekend, its dramatic sign, and the assurance that I was following the direction of God.

In the coming years I would graduate from college, then complete seminary. I have experienced great joy along the way. Where the need was, there was also the joy of service. I have walked a long way with God at my side. These years of service have been rich treasures.

Genesis 12:1-4. Now the Lord said to Abram, Go from your country and your kindred and your father's house to the land that I will show you. . . . I will bless you. . . . So Abram went, as the Lord had told him.

8

A Seminary
Education by Degrees

*I could not admit, at this stage of life,
my call to the ministry.*

I have friends who graduated from college with a Bible degree, then entered seminary and three years later had their M.Div. This was not my experience.

My major in college was psychology because I could not at that stage of life admit to family and friends that I felt called to prepare for the ministry. I grew up in an era when most ministers were chosen by lot, and I was afraid it would seem presumptuous to admit to a special calling.

Following graduation from Eastern Mennonite College, I enrolled as a first-year seminary student at Union Theological Seminary in Richmond, Virginia. I loved the Presbyterian emphasis on God's grace. My student internship was served under Dr. John Brown at Ginter Park Presbyterian Church.

We expected to settle down for three years of study. But at the end of my first year at Union, I had the opportunity to become campus pastor at my alma mater. Knowing the opening would not be there if I waited to complete seminary, I decided to accept the position. Our family moved back to the Valley.

From then on, my seminary training would be piecemeal. As full-time pastor of students, I could take one class each semester at Eastern Mennonite Seminary. In the summer months I studied at Union Theological Seminary in New York City. By spring 1969, Eastern Mennonite Seminary pulled all the credits together and granted my M.Div.

Looking back on this drawn-out study, it seems to me that I received many extra blessings and that the diversity has been enriching. At Union in Richmond, I heard world-renowned Karl Barth speak to the student body. During a question-and-answer period in the crowded student lounge, I found a place to sit on the floor "at his feet." Barth was asked to put his theology into a few simple words. He responded, "Jesus loves me this I know."

At Union in New York City, I saw in the grand hallways theologian Paul Tillich in conversation with Abraham Heschel, who taught at the neighboring Jewish Theological Seminary.

Also in New York City, at the Riverside Church next to Union, I heard Martin Luther King Jr. preach. I had to stand in line and was one of the last allowed to enter the church that morning.

Back at Eastern Mennonite Seminary, I became acquainted with Martin Marty and Mark Hatfield. Marty even stayed in our home for a week! What a perfect guest he was. He played with our children. He was interested in our everyday life.

A few days after Marty left, we received in the mail a package of books—for Kathy *Little Girl in the Valley*; for Don a book about baseball; for Betty a book of German verse, and for me one of Marty's well-written theology books.

I have been supremely blessed with great teachers, thoughtful mentors, and wonderful books. On my desk is a bookmark with a quote by Thomas Jefferson: "I cannot live without books." This could be my own statement.

9

Ordination, a Sacred Privilege

Awesome responsibilities were placed on my shoulders.

It was an honor to be invited back to Eastern Mennonite College to serve as campus pastor. I loved the idea of working with students at a time when they were making important choices and becoming the next generation of leaders.

Immediately after I accepted the position, President Myron Augsburger set the wheels turning for my ordination. This request was approved by Virginia Conference, the Mennonite denominational body charged with overseeing such matters, and it was decided that I should be ordained in my home congregation, the Warwick River Mennonite Church.

In the days and weeks leading up to the ordination service, I did a lot of soul-searching. I sensed that my "Yes" was followed by the "Yes" of Christ.

Pastors are expected to live exemplary lives and remain true to their calling for life. It seemed like a huge expectation. I believed that Jesus would be with me and would give me the power to live my ordination vows. I would not have to walk alone.

In May 1964, on a Sunday evening, Myron Augsburger preached the sermon. Then it was time for me to kneel and take my vows.

I remember the hands of the bishops on my head—heavy hands, placing on my shoulders awesome responsibilities. I remember their prayers, asking that I be blessed by the Holy Spirit. I felt that the place I knelt was holy ground. And then the hands that had seemed to be so heavy were lifting me up.

In the days that followed, I remember thinking, *Who will I model my ministry after? Whom do I admire and want to follow?* There were many mentors and ministers I appreciated. Then I began to realize that ministry must be modeled after Jesus Christ himself. It was Jesus who took a basin and towel and washed his disciples' feet. I was being ordained to become a servant of God's people.

I have tried to learn the way of discipleship and obedience. Somewhere in my journey, I became tuned in to the writings of Henri Nouwen. His book, *The Wounded Healer,* offers many insights. I realize that Jesus was a wounded healer—that by his stripes all of us are healed.

I would do it all again. It has been a sacred privilege to live the life of one called and ordained by Christ and his church.

10

President Myron Augsburger's Fast Pace

I heard a scratching noise coming from the trunk.

Without trying to be nosy, we could see Myron's comings and goings. Myron could do two or three or four things at once. When I moved from the Tidewater area of Virginia to be campus pastor at Eastern Mennonite College at college president Myron's invitation, our family moved into a house across the road from Myron and Esther and their family.

It seemed to me that Myron ran at a fast and furious pace. I was more at home with the slower pace of the South. I wonder what my industrious neighbors thought of my slower movements. If I came home for lunch, I came to eat and rest. I would see Myron striding toward the house for his lunch break, but on the way up the walk he would bend over and push three little acorns into the ground. No wonder he was president and I wasn't!

Oh well, I preferred being campus pastor. What a wonderful first pastorate! It was the opportunity of a lifetime, I believed, to relate to hundreds of college students. My parishioners were young, studious, and excited about life. It was such a wonderful place to work that I continued in the role for thirteen years.

One spring, just before graduation, Jonathan Kanagy, a member of the senior class, was badly injured in a motorcycle accident and taken to the University Hospital in Charlottesville. For weeks they kept him immobile, trying to save his leg. As we came closer to the day of graduation, it occurred to me that if Jonathan could not come to the college to pick up his degree, then the college must go to Jonathan.

It was all arranged—President Augsburger and four student leaders would accompany me to the hospital, and we would hold our own little ceremony and would award the degree. Early one Saturday morning, Myron picked me up. Then we stopped at the dorm for the students who would ride along.

A little ways down the road, I heard a scratching noise coming from the trunk of Myron's car. I asked, "What's that strange sound?"

Myron replied, "Two swans are in the trunk. They've been ordered for weeks, and I haven't had time to deliver them!"

We arrived at the edge of Charlottesville and drove through the gates of the beautiful Boar's Head Inn. Myron, who raised swans, jumped from the car, opened the trunk, carried the cage to the lake, and pushed the two elegant swans into the water. We drove on to the hospital and enjoyed a meaningful time with Jonathan.

Mission accomplished. Or, shall I say, missions accomplished! Myron marched to a different drummer.

11

Loren Swartzendruber's Inaugural Lunch

"They wanted some guy named Reverend."

I met Loren thirty years ago. At that time he was working in the Eastern Mennonite College Admissions Office. One day, in the old library-turned-office, this prediction was overheard: "Someday Loren Swartzendruber will be president of Hesston College and later will become president of Eastern Mennonite College."

Pat, of course, has been part of this amazing story. When they were both students at Iowa Mennonite High School, they couldn't help but notice each other. They spent a lot of time together. Following high school graduation, they went their separate ways. Pat entered nurses training and Loren enrolled as a freshman at Eastern Mennonite. That year they became engaged.

During his years at Eastern Mennonite, Loren became an associate in campus ministries. We had good times working together on campus church committee. Loren was full of youthful energy and had a strong sense of direction for his life.

It was an honor to be invited to Lower Deer Creek Church in Iowa for Loren's ordination to the ministry. Our daughter Kathleen remembers this trip to Iowa. It was the middle of the growing season. All we could see were cornfields, and we weren't sure we would ever find the church.

We have remained friends with Loren and Pat and their family. In 2002, when Eastern Mennonite University (formerly Eastern Mennonite College) started looking for a new president, we learned that Loren was being considered for the position. We then welcomed the announcement that he had been chosen.

A few weeks before the inauguration, I was asked to share stories about his life. This gave me reason to contact old friends and family members. A story I particularly enjoyed: Loren's son remembers the time his five-year-old sister ran to answer the phone and with a puzzled look on her face said, "You must have the wrong number." Returning to the table, she explained, "They wanted some guy named Reverend Swartzendruber."

"Friends" at Mennonite Board of Education tell this story: Once Loren flew to a speaking engagement at a conservative church. He went to pick up the rental car at the airport and was quite disturbed to find that the only car available was a big, black, shiny Lincoln Continental.

This would never do! Loren protested. After a lengthy argument he was offered a Ford. This felt much better—until the Ford showed up. It was a red Mustang convertible.

I have learned to know a lot of Iowa folks, and I have come to this observation: "Can anything but good come out of Iowa?"

12

A Guide
for the Journey

Three days passed, and I received a call.

I loved working with young people. They were so full of energy and enthusiasm and creativity. I remember saying that I could never enjoy being pastor to the parents as much as I had enjoyed being pastor to their children. But now I had been pastor of college students for twelve years, and it was time for me to move on.

John Moseman was a Spirit-filled man who had been pastor of the Goshen (Ind.) College Congregation. Because of his unusual gifts of discernment and vision, our denomination had appointed him as a clearinghouse for pastors in transition. He regularly sent out an information sheet listing available pastors. I called John. It was not my desire to be on the list, but I did want to have a conversation with John. I told him I was considering leaving the campus. Would he know of any openings? I asked him to keep me in his thoughts and prayers as he heard about the needs of congregations. Maybe something would click.

Three days passed. Finally I received a call from John. As he considered our conversation, two congregations kept coming to mind: The Akron congregation and the Blooming Glen congregation, both located in Pennsylvania, were searching for pastors. I gave John permission to share my name with the Akron congregation. I had visited there, liked the people, and thought it would be a place I could serve.

The very next evening Urbane Peachey, chair of the Akron search committee, called. We arranged a meeting with the committee. The invitation was issued and we spent the next eight years in this wonderful church. Many miracles happened. It was the right place!

A number of years later, during a brief period of serving in our home church in Virginia, we received a call from Paul Lederach, overseer of Blooming Glen Church in Bucks County, Pennsylvania. Would I consider serving as pastor at Blooming Glen? I spent the next ten years there. Again it seemed an answer to prayer.

Reflecting on my journey, I thank God for people like John Moseman who have been guides along the way. I was led to wonderful places of service. I am reminded of Psalm 32:8:"I will instruct you and teach you the way you should go. I will counsel you with my eye upon you."

13

A Valuable Lesson

Should we take our toys and go home?

Before we arrived at our first church in Pennsylvania, we received several phone calls from one of the small groups in the church, inviting us to be part of their group. They sounded like a fun group—about our age, with children the ages of our two.

Still, we hesitated. We were not sure a pastor should be part of a small group within the congregation. We had heard various opinions on the subject. Some believed a pastor should only be in a group outside his parish

We decided to accept this group's invitation. They did neat things—played tennis, ate dinner in each other's homes, and studied books together. We were pretty sure it was the right thing to do. They didn't make us feel we were different just because of the pastoral role. In fact, one of the women in the group was enrolled at the local seminary. Her interest in theology sparked many of our group conversations.

Anna would graduate from seminary our third year at Akron. Her graduation would happen about the same time as our son's graduation from Hesston College. It would be a month of celebrations. It looked like we could make our trip to Kansas, bring Don home, and be back in time to attend Anna's festivities. We had learned that Anna's best friend was hosting a party following the graduation ceremonies.

When the time came to drive to Hesston, we still had not received our invitation to the party. Eventually it sank in. All the rest of our small group had their invitations, but we were not going to be invited!

We felt hurt, dismayed, and rejected, with a huge cloud over our heads. Betty called her counselor cousin in Virginia and told Danny about this big party we were being excluded from. By this time we had learned that it was a wine and cheese party. Over the phone Danny got the picture and was full of suggestions: "On the evening of the party, go out and get drunk, appear on the host's doorstep with a block of cheese, and say, 'We were afraid you thought we didn't like cheese.'"

A friend who was a retired pastor listened to my grumbling. Upon hearing my sad story of exclusion and disappointment in my church friends, he said, "It sounds as though you'd like to take your toys and go home." Then he added, "If Anna had to invite you to her party, then you couldn't be her pastor."

This started to make sense. It was one more valuable lesson we had to learn about this pastor role. We would be included in some of the celebration activities of our church family, but there would be times of being held at arm's length. It goes with the territory! We've been able to look back over similar times and say to ourselves, "They did us a favor to leave us off the guest list."

14

Coffee with the Pastor

*"In my crisis, the church kicked me out,
leaving me hurt and angry."*

The church was large, and it seemed I would never learn to know its partcipants on a personal basis. I was not comfortable being pastor to people I had never even talked with. I had attended funerals at which I would hear a minister say, "I really didn't know 'Susan' that well." Something was wrong with that picture.

I came upon an idea. I had never heard of such a plan, but I wanted to try it. On Sunday morning, I explained that I would like an hour with every member. I suggested that we call it "Coffee with the Pastor." A voice piped up in the congregation, "Would Elfrieda and I come together?"

I was ready for Peter! I replied, "No, because you would do all the talking and she wouldn't get a chance." We all laughed.

From the church office we sent an invitation to all members, asking them to suggest times that might fit their week. The response was overwhelmingly positive. The church secretary would make the appointments; we were able to arrange at least five "coffees" each week. What a rewarding experience it was for me! What a difference it made in ministering to this group of people.

Funny things along the way kept things lively. On one occasion the reply card was signed by a stranger. This person was not on our list. Was somebody playing a trick? I picked up the telephone, dialed the number, and explained that I was responding to her request for an hour with the pastor. She hooted at me that she had *not* filled out any card and was *not* interested in a one-on-one with a pastor.

Then a light bulb must have come on, and she chuckled. "I think I know what happened! My brother goes to your church. He's always worrying about me and my salvation!"

We chatted another minute, and I started to close our conversation as gracefully as possible.

But she interrupted, "You know, I would like to make this appointment. I have not been to church for nearly forty years."

She drove twenty miles to the church and was on time. At first she tested me with her outbursts and her four-letter-words. She had a lot to say about churches and pastors and bishops.

Then she told her story: "From my infancy, my family was part of an ultra-conservative church. As a young adult I joined the church, but I was rather wild and dated a lot of guys. At seventeen I was pregnant."

By now she was shedding tears. "Right when I needed the church they excommunicated me. They kicked me out. I have been angry at the church ever since."

Long pause. "There is one memory from the experience that has stayed with me through the years. The bishop who read my letter of excommunication wept the whole time he read it."

Through my years as a pastor I've met so many who have been wounded by their church. I pray that God will grant me the grace to reach out to those who have been hurt. I want to read the Bible through new glasses and with a new heart! I firmly believe that the church is a hospital for sinners, not a hotel for saints.

Coffee with the pastor was one of the best discoveries of my ministry. I ended up hosting hundreds of these one-on-one visits, mostly in my office at the church. We could meet with no television or radio blaring, no family interruptions, just a private conversation between two people in a quiet setting. Honest confessions were made, tears shed, transformations undergone.

During these sacred times, I felt more energized, more inspired, more alive than at any other time. I need to know my people!

> *James 5:16.* Confess your sins to one another, and pray for one another, so that you may be healed. The prayer of the righteous is powerful and effective.

15

The Pastor's Family Needs a Pastor

We drove all night, drinking coffee and talking to stay awake.

It was Friday evening, and we were looking forward to a special weekend. Kathleen and her new husband Dean were coming from Indiana to Pennsylvania to visit us. They had left right after work and would get to our place after midnight.

I always feel some anxiety when a family member is on the highway. Until her safe arrival I would be unsettled and preoccupied. About 8:00 p.m. the phone rang. Kathy.

She assured me they were safe, but there had been an accident. When they were about a hundred miles from home, the roads were slick from a wintry mix and a horse had suddenly appeared in the middle of the road. Kathy swerved to miss the horse, and the car flipped over on its roof.

First of all, we gave thanks that our children were not harmed, just shaken and scared. Next we admitted how disappointed we were to not see them. Then one of us said, "Why don't we go to Indiana to be sure they are okay?"

Within the hour we were ready to leave. I called somebody and asked that person to take charge at Sunday morning services. We left a message on Kathy's phone saying that we were coming. We drove all night, drinking coffee and talking to keep each other awake, and arrived at the kids' apartment by mid-morning.

It was comforting to spend the next hours with Kathy and Dean. We got to hear firsthand about the broken fence and the horse that got out of his field. We talked about what they could do for transportation until insurance details could be worked out. We had a relaxing day together.

Next morning, we were enjoying a leisurely breakfast when the phone rang. It was our good friend, Ura Gingerich, explaining that he and Gladys were in Goshen and had heard about the accident. He offered to look up the address and find us at our daughter's place.

When Ura and Gladys walked through the door, I was hit with a flood of relief.

Ura listened patiently to all the details of the accident, letting us go over and over the fears and concerns and also the thankfulness that nobody was hurt.

He even had us huddle in a circle while he prayed for our well-being. Ura had become our pastor!

Before the two of them left, I saw Ura talking privately with Dean and Kathy. Later we learned that he had offered them an interest-free loan so they could buy another car. They accepted the offer with relief and gratitude. In the coming months we often heard them talk with or about Ura as a wonderful friend in time of need.

This is one of the many times we learned that pastors need pastors. A congregation is truly blessed to have members like Ura and Gladys who care deeply for the needs of others and who are not afraid to extend themselves to help.

16

Generous Jody

*She covered for me, making me
look better than I was.*

When we moved to Blooming Glen, I became acquainted
with the best group of elders ever to serve a church. In
addition, I fell heir to the best administrative assistant in history. Jody retired from school teaching when her children were
young. When she decided to reenter the workplace, she accepted the part-time job at the church. For Jody it was a calling.

I happen to know that in later years, when she was told that
she should consider going into the ministry, she would always
reply, "I have found my ministry."

Jody wanted the church to look good in the community,
and she wanted the pastors to look good. Countless times,
often when I wasn't even aware of it, she was covering for me
and making me look good. Better than I was.

For one thing, committee meetings for me could be a real
chore. There was not only the meeting itself but the endless
phone calls and memos following the meeting to communicate
with people regarding assignments and requests for help.

In previous churches, it was up to me to make those phone
calls. If I procrastinated, as I was prone to do, the job would get

bigger, and sometimes this lack of communication was downright embarrassing.

Imagine my delight at hearing Jody taking on these responsibilities. During the committee meeting, she was so knowledgeable about the congregation that she seemed to know in advance who would accept a particular assignment.

On leaving the meeting, she could be heard on her phone in the next office. In a positive, affirming manner she could make a request, expect a positive response, and usually get a yes. Jody seemed to have all the calls made by the time the committee members left the building.

The gift of her support was not an occasional thing. I found out that she did things daily for the church that made us all happier and the church office a smoothly functioning place.

During our ten years at this church, Jody became a wonderful friend and colleague. If there was anything she loved more than the church, it was her own husband and children.

I was asked to participate in the wedding of her daughter Cher and Doug. How well I remember that evening of celebration. Bruce had the yard and grounds looking like the Garden of Eden. We celebrated bonds of love with a beautiful couple, but more than that, bonds of love in a community of beloved family and friends. I was honored to serve at such a time.

Years later, when I had returned to Virginia, Jody called with the good news, "Caleb has found the perfect woman! They will be married at her home in Florida. Would you be willing to meet with Caleb and Jennie to do their premarital counseling?" We met and had a profitable, relaxing afternoon together, talking about pitfalls to avoid and ways to become soulmates.

When I remember my time at Blooming Glen, I remember many, many miracles. Jody was one of the miracles.

17

A Mennonite Police Chief

He promised his mother
never to point a gun at a human.

George and Nancy had been attending the church for ten years. They made a great addition—both were well-known and respected in the community. George was chief of police, and Nancy was a nurse supervisor at the local hospital.

One morning, a call came from George explaining that Nancy had just received results from medical tests, and the diagnosis was cancer. They were devastated. Would I come and pray with them? Of course I would. I asked if I could bring along Harold, their good friend and neighboring farmer.

Together the four of us knelt to pray. We poured out our hearts asking for a miracle. As we stood together, I took Nancy's hand and assured her of the church's great love for the family and that we would commit ourselves to ongoing prayer. Then I added, "It would be such a blessing for you and George to come into membership in our congregation."

Even while I spoke, I asked myself, *Could I be in trouble here? These folks have been attending for years, and is there a reason they have not become members?*

Our church took a strong stand against guns and violence. Would a police chief belong in a "peace" church?" Would the elders say I had overstepped my privileges? I was assaulted by doubts.

Two weeks later, following the benediction, George was the first to greet me at the front of the church, announcing, "Nancy and I would like to pursue membership." Surely this was good news! But what if someone objected?

In the coming days and weeks, George told me his story. When he was still a young man, the local chief of police approached him and explained, "We are looking for some clean-cut young men to join our force."

When George reported this conversation to his parents, his Mennonite father gave his consent. His German Reformed mother was reluctant, saying, "I don't think a Christian should carry a gun."

After giving it a lot of prayerful consideration, George made a promise to his mother. He promised that, although he would have to carry a gun, he would never point it toward a human being. His parents were satisfied and gave their blessing. Forty years later, George was telling me that he had kept his promise.

George and Nancy joined the membership class, testifying of their faith in God and their desire to join themselves to Blooming Glen Mennonite Church. Their classmates heard George's story of being an officer who kept the peace. Then the whole church heard their story.

On a beautiful Sunday morning, George and Nancy knelt in the front of the church and were baptized. Miracles happen! There were no objections—only a warm welcome from all the church family.

18

Stitched Together in Love

As his eyesight decreased, the size of his stitches increased.

"Did he make 100 blankets?" the first child asked.

"More than that," I replied.

"Two hundred?" "Five hundred?" "A thousand?"

"More than that," I kept replying.

On this cold December morning, I walked to the front of Neffsville Mennonite Church, wearing a homemade comforter on my shoulders, and invited the children to come forward for the children's story.

I explained that Simon Smoker, a member of our church, made 15,000 comforters for homeless people. Sim (that's what everyone called him) lived to be an old man. For many years he stayed at home to care for his invalid wife. He would dress Irene, feed her, and put her to bed. He had to do everything for her because she was not able to take care of herself.

It could not have been easy being at home all day taking care of his wife. But Sim gave thanks for his warm and cozy home. And he started thinking of people around the world who had no home and no warm place to stay. He thought to himself,

I could make blankets for cold people. I could do that right here in my own home, even while I am taking care of Irene.

So that's exactly what Sim did. He gathered together all the fabric he could find in his own home. His friends brought him boxes of fabric they had stored in their attics. He bought a sewing machine and learned how to use the machine.

For twenty years he cared for his wife and made comforters for the homeless. He delivered the finished blankets to Mennonite Central Committee (MCC) and sometimes took home more fabric to make the next blankets. After his wife died, he continued to make blankets.

Some of the children knew that Sim had now gone to heaven. The representative from MCC, Leone Wagner, came to pay tribute to Sim and brought one of his last comforters to his memorial service at the church.

She had this to say about Sim: "As Sim got older he had to stop using his sewing machine and instead sewed the pieces together by hand. As his eyesight decreased, the size of his stitches increased."

She also explained, "Sometimes Sim joked about his color combinations. He said the sewing circle ladies didn't always like the way he made blankets.

Do you think it mattered to the cold and homeless person on the street?

I don't think so either. You know what I think happened after Sim died? I think he heard the voice of God saying,

Come, you who are blessed by my Father. . . .
I was hungry and you gave me something to eat,
I was thirsty and you gave me something to drink. . . .
I needed clothes and you clothed me.
I was sick and you looked after me.

Simon Smoker will be remembered for his kindness and generosity and his unselfish desire to follow the example of Jesus. What a model he is for all of us!

19

White-Water Rafting

*Unplanned happenings seem
to go with camp life.*

The summer of 1972 we were serving as resource people for
Family Week at Laurelville Church Camp. Jim and
Thelma Brunk were on duty as medical personnel, and Betty
and I were to have the "spiritual input." Every day was packed
with planned activities (and the unplanned happenings that
seem to go with camp life.)

Toward the end of the week, the scheduled activities included a rafting trip on the Monongahela River. We had never
been on such an expedition and were eager to go. We would
enjoy being off-duty, away from camp, with the river guides in
charge.

About twenty-five people signed up for the trip. Our group
was divided, and we boarded onto four or five rafts, with an experienced guide in the lead. The trip down the river was expected to take several hours, then we would be picked up by
more guides who would bring us back to the original starting
point.

The river was calm, the sun was shining on the rippling
water, and we were in high spirits. The rafts drifted aimlessly
along. It seemed like the perfect time for a nap. I laid my head

on the side of the raft—no responsibility, no worry, the perfect moment.

I woke to shouts and screams.

We had entered the white water!

The raft twisted and turned and tilted,

a camera fell overboard,

a woman was

thrown into the churning river!

The husband grabbed the leg of his wife and hauled her back into the raft. I found an oar and tried to help stabilize our craft. We hung on for dear life. Just as fast as we had hit the rapids, we were suddenly out of them. The water was smooth and we settled into the quiet stillness of a perfectly calm river. We stopped for lunch along the banks. We were proud to have braved the wild rapids.

I like the image of "white-water faith." It is not stagnant or stale—it is faith in action!

Pascal referred to the quiet waters in his writings:

Nothing is so insufferable to man as to be completely at rest, without passions, without business, without diversion, without study. He then feels his nothingness, his forlornness, his insufficiency, his dependence, his weakness, his emptiness.

We are called to risk and excitement, testing and survival. Then our hearts beat with excitement and challenge. Jesus and those around him were white-water people. They lived by faith and trust in a white-water God!

20

God's Teachable Children (Sermon)

Moldable, forgiving, trusting, pure, free to hurt and cry, laugh and grow.

"Truly I tell you," says Jesus in Matthew 18:3, "unless you change and become like children, you will never enter the kingdom of heaven."

What is it about children that causes Jesus to hold them up as
        models for his people?
Is it their size?
    Children are little,
            Powerless,
                Vulnerable,
                    Dependent,
                        Soft and gentle.
Is it their innocence?
    Children are pure,
            Unmarred,
                Without malice,

Without evil,
    Trusting and honest.
Is it because they ask tough questions?
    Children are not afraid to ask questions.
        They catch us off guard with their perceptions.
Is it the "natural" feelings of love and protection we have for small
    children?
        We hold them close.
            We feel affectionate and tender.
                We maintain eye contact.
Remember our first days of school?
    So eager to learn.
    Wanting to drink it all in.
    Listening with rapt attention.
    Trusting and respecting.
    Responding.
And then we become adults—
    Our minds start closing up,
    We become resistant and defensive:
    Don't tell me!
    Hard-headed like a three foot wall which cannot be broken
        through.

There seems to be this pattern in all living things, to start off open, responsive, vulnerable, eager to learn. Then with a little bit of age and a little bit of maturity, to begin closing up, resisting knowledge, becoming dogmatic and hard-headed, wearing tough armament.

Like a kitten,
    Playful and soft,
        A purring, touchable bundle of fur.
            A lovely little kitten!
Six months later the kitten is a cat with claws,
    Arched back,

Eyes that stare you down,
   Scratching and hostile.
      A scary old cat!
No wonder Jesus said, "Unless you change and become like children you will never enter the kingdom of heaven."

Unless you become moldable like a child,
   open and receptive,
Unless you become forgiving like a child,
   holding no grudges,
Unless you become trusting like a child,
   believing God is in control without needing to understand,
Unless you become pure like a child,
   harboring no malice or condescending, self-serving pride,
Unless you become free as a child,
   free to hurt and cry,
      free to laugh and grow,
         free to try and fail—
You will never enter the kingdom of heaven.

21

The Joy of Baptism

Ricky had always wanted to pour water on his sister. Now he laughed.

Our denomination has a strong background in believers' baptism. This is not interpreted the same by all pastors or youth leaders. Some feel that the person must be able to understand all the responsibility that goes with baptism and be mature enough to make a careful and serious lifetime commitment. Others hold that young believers should be baptized when they first hear the call of Jesus and decide they want to be a Christian.

Parents, too, differ widely on this question of when their children should be baptized. Some young parents are anxious to see their child take the step of baptism and church membership. Other parents hope their child will be satisfied to wait until a more mature commitment can be made.

At one church, I followed a pastor who had been at the church for ten years and had emphasized the call to a commitment of maturity and costly discipleship. As a result, there were about twenty young people who had graduated from high school, were now away at college, and were still waiting to take this step of believer's baptism. Together with the parents and youth leaders, we worked hard to invite this group who had skipped baptism. Eventually, most of them made the decision to be baptized.

I have noticed that sometime in the early teens, a child often has a tender conscience that makes it possible to hear the invitation of Jesus. Young people will tell about a campfire experience at which Jesus' voice spoke clearly and they responded.

When I hear this kind of confession, I like to tell the young person, "You don't have to have all the answers at this point. You don't have to be perfect to be baptized. You will make many mistakes. Baptism is the beginning of a lifetime journey."

One particular baptism I will always remember. At the appointed time, Linda came with her parents and siblings to the front of the church. Linda gave a beautiful testimony, then answered the usual questions and knelt to receive baptism. I released a generous handful of water over her head, saying, "Linda, upon the confession you have made to God and to this congregation, I baptize you with water in the name of the Father, Son, and Holy Spirit."

Uncontrollable giggling, hysterical and unstoppable, came from her younger brother. It was too much! Ricky had always wanted to pour water on his sister; now it was happening. A preacher and a congregation made it all the more hilarious.

Baptism is often a time for tears of joy. This time it was an occasion for hilarity.

At every baptism, I believe that the heavens open up, and a voice says, "You are my beloved child. I am well pleased with you."

22

Please Accept Me

*If you join our church, we'll give you a
copy of the Mennonite cookbook.*

Every morning Jane dropped off her son at the door of the
school next to the church. Warwick River Christian School
is owned by the church. The teachers are dedicated Christians
and create a wonderful climate for a child's development.

Local families, many of them military families living near
the church, seem to want their children to attend our school. It
is always the hope of our local church that the families bringing
their children will also feel drawn to be part of our church. But
this does not usually happen.

On this particular morning, after dropping off Don, Jane
decided to come into the church and find somebody to talk
with. This would be the first of many conversations between
Jane and me in the coming months. We talked about the basic
foundations of our church and the church Jane had been part
of.

Before we got very far, Jane said, "I would never be allowed
to join your church. I have too much history. I would be unac-
ceptable." She began telling her story. She was in her third marriage. Her second marriage produced son Don, now in sixth
grade in our school.

Her first marriage, to which five children were born, ended when her pastor-husband left her. That split was so hurtful and so emotional it could not be told without tears. Some of her children had decided to stay with their father and were alienated from Jane.

Lately I had been reminding the church members that "Church needs to be a hospital for sinners, not a hotel for saints." So when Jane repeated that our church would never accept her, I replied, "Why don't you give us a try? Would you be interested in coming to our small group and getting to know a few of us?" She accepted the invitation and came to the group.

In a few weeks she brought husband Walter along. In the context of the small group, where each member had an evening to tell life stories, Jane decided that it was time to tell her journey. She wept, and we all wept with her. She had experienced so much heartache.

After years of alienation from church, Jane experienced the cleansing that comes with confession, and our group experienced a sense of closeness and understanding and bonding that was new for us.

Jane and Walter became regular members of the small group. As Jane began expressing interest in joining the larger church, some in the group would say, "If you join our church, we will give you the *Mennonite Cookbook!*" In a few months, with all the small group members huddled around them in the front of the church, the couple received baptism. What a day of rejoicing it was!

At the end of the service, somebody from the small group handed Jane a beautifully wrapped copy of Mary Emma Showalter's *Mennonite Cookbook.*

23

A Last Visit
with Uncle George

*As a tent evangelist, he sometimes preached
to crowds of ten thousand.*

Uncle George was ninety years old and had been in and out of the hospital. He was growing weaker, and family members were saying good-bye. So many people wanted a last word with him, and his caretakers had to pace these visits. I called my cousin Rowland Shank, and he agreed to go with me to make this last call on our uncle.

Uncle George was a big man and had a big reputation. As a tent evangelist, he would sometimes speak to crowds of ten thousand. Throughout my own ministry, countless people have told tell me they became Christian in one of Uncle George's meetings.

I was not always comfortable with Uncle George. Maybe I felt a little guilty around him. Maybe he would discover that I needed to walk the sawdust trail. We were never too close, not like some uncles and nephews.

But once when we were talking together, Uncle George said, "I could never do what you do in your working individually with people." That was high praise from Uncle George.

Surely he knew I had always thought that I could never speak in public the way he did.

Rowland and I waited in the living room, then it was our turn to see Uncle George. We had a short visit and talked about our common roots. George was alert. I asked, "Uncle George, can we have a prayer before we go?" Uncle George loved prayer and readily agreed.

I began praying in generalities, then felt the Spirit tell me to be specific. I prayed, "Dear Lord, Uncle George loves to preach. He will soon be in heaven with you. Could you arrange for him to preach to the saints in heaven?"

I can easily imagine that Uncle George is standing and preaching to the largest crowd ever! He is at home and God himself is adding the "Amens."

A Text for a Sermon in Heaven

Worthy is the Lamb that was
*   slaughtered*
to receive power and wealth and
*   wisdom and might*
and honor and glory and blessing.
—Revelation 5:12

24

Hunter Hears the Call

*His grandfather always turned
the conversation to spiritual things.*

In recent years I enjoy the privilege of connecting with students at nearby Eastern Mennonite Seminary. Sometimes I lead a class of first-year students in their small group activities.

This year I have been working with seniors who are finishing their formal education and receiving calls from churches. What an exciting time for these seminarians and their families. It is exhilarating to help prepare the next generation of dedicated men and women who are hearing the call and saying "Yes."

Hunter is one of these persons responding to God's call. And it has been especially meaningful to me to relate to Hunter because I have known his grandparents and great-grandparents. J. L. Stauffer, past president of Eastern Mennonite College, was a big man and one of my professors in the Bible department. J. Mark Stauffer, Hunter's grandfather, was the head of the music department, directing all the major choirs during my early years on campus.

During his years at Warwick High School in Lititz, Pennsylvania, Hunter was an outstanding athlete. He was a football player, an offensive end, and he was good. College coaches noticed his game skills, and he was offered a scholarship to Ithaca College in New York.

For a number of years, Hunter was not much interested in the church, but he did occasionally attend his home church, Neffsville Mennonite Church in Lancaster. He remembers that Pastor Linford King took a special interest in him and was the source of a lot of affirmation and encouragement.

Hunter grew up in a home divided by divorce. Both parents have continued to show him their love and support and both of them give Hunter their blessing in their own ways.

For example, Hunter's mother, Marti, buys him expensive suits when she finds them at special prices. During his student years, this might not have seemed so important. But as he steps into his first pastorate, Hunter will discover that a good suit can take a big hunk out of his salary.

While Hunter was finishing his college education, he would often drive on Interstate 81 past Chambersburg, Pennsylvania, and would stop to see his grandparents. Eva and J. Mark Stauffer were now living at Menno Haven, where J. Mark was chaplain.

Hunter remembers that his grandfather always turned the conversation to spiritual things. One day his grandfather asked, "Have you ever been baptized?" Hunter replied that he was a believer but he had never been baptized and would like to be.

Grandfather J. Mark went to the kitchen and came back with a bowl of water. Hunter knelt on the living room carpet and was baptized by his beloved grandfather.

God has been watching over Hunter and has called him by name. Hunter and Grace have listened and heard and said "Yes." The young husband and wife and tiny daughter, Olivia, moved to Souderton, Pennsylvania, to accept the call of Zion Mennonite Church. God moves in miraculous ways his church to build.

Credits

Note: The author has attempted to secure permission for telling stories of any persons named in this book. In some cases he has changed names to protect identities.

Pt 1., ch. 8. "Waiting," George R. Brunk, excerpted from *The Centerpoint: Personal Reflections of George R. Brunk I.* Harrisonburg, Va.: The Sword and Trumpet, Inc., 1992.

Pt. 1, ch. 8. "A Call for Help," J. B. Smith, *Church and Sunday School Hymnal.* Scottdale, Pa.: Mennonite Publishing House, 1902. Public domain.

Pt. 1, ch. 9. "Remember Me," John S. Coffman. *Church and Sunday School Hymnal,* public domain.

Pt. 1, ch. 10. "A Covenant Prayer in the Wesley Tradition," is a Pietist prayer adapted by John Wesley. Public domain.

Pt. 1, ch. 21. "My Life Flows On," Robert Lowry, 1869. Permission granted to use by Brethren Press, Elgin, Ill.

Pt. 1, ch. 25. "O Little Town of Bethlehem," Phillips Brooks, 1874, is in public domain. The lines from "an ancient poet" are in public domain, widely quoted, and sometimes identified as being by an anonymous fifteenth-century (or other century) poet.

Pt. 3, ch. 1. "How Firm a Foundation," John Rippon, 1787. Public domain.

The Author

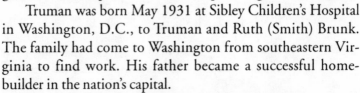

Truman H. Brunk, retired pastor, lives in Harrisonburg, Virginia, on an acre plot with three sheep and eight fruit trees.

Truman was born May 1931 at Sibley Children's Hospital in Washington, D.C., to Truman and Ruth (Smith) Brunk. The family had come to Washington from southeastern Virginia to find work. His father became a successful home-builder in the nation's capital.

After the crash of 1929, when the home-buyers moved out and let their houses go back to the builder, Truman's parents, now deeply in debt, left Washington and moved their family to the Mennonite Colony in Warwick County, Virginia, to be near grandparents and start over.

His parents planted forty acres of peach and apple trees and dreamed of the day they would be debt-free. Truman has good memories of working with his parents in the orchard. He and his mother sold peaches along Duke of Gloucester Street in Williamsburg, where one customer was John D. Rockefeller.

Truman attended Denbigh Elementary School. Then he was sent to Eastern Mennonite High School in Harrisonburg, Virginia, graduating in 1949. Later he graduated from Eastern

Mennonite College (now University) and Eastern Mennonite Seminary. He also studied at Union Theological Seminary in Richmond and in New York.

Since his ordination in 1965 and his twelve years as campus pastor at EMC, Truman has served as pastor in five locations: Akron Mennonite Church in Lancaster County, Pennsylvania; Blooming Glen Mennonite Church in Bucks County, Pennsylvania; Warwick River Mennonite Church in Newport News, Virginia; and associate pastor at Harrisonburg Mennonite Church in Harrisonburg, Virginia.

Recently he and Betty have served as interim pastors, including at Neffsville Mennonite Church in Lancaster, Pennsylvania. Along with pastoral duties, Truman has been overseer for churches in Pennsylvania and Virginia.

Before his church work, Truman built houses in the Newport News area. In 1952 he married his childhood sweetheart, Elizabeth (Betty) Shenk. They are parents of two adult children: Kathleen, married to Dean Isaacs, lives in Waterville, Ohio, with their two teenage children, Andrew and Adrienne; and Don, married to Deb Clemens, lives in Souderton, Pennsylvania, with their two sons, Caleb and Isaac.

Reflecting on his life—working in the orchard, building homes, pastoring, everything he's ever done—Truman would do it all again.

Printed in the United States
73576LV00002BA/352-354